Silk On Fire

The Ultimate Guide On Craving Sex With Your Husband

by Karen Moilliet

2013

Table of Contents

Special Thanks

I AM DEEPLY GRATEFUL for my parents, who instilled in me a healthy attitude toward my sexuality.

My deepest thanks to my husband, Ian, my champion: because of him, my story is filled with success and joy.

I want to thank all my friends who gave me their stories; their valued time in reading and critiquing my manuscript in its rawest form and their ideas for book covers and titles.

I would not be on this journey if I had not been blessed with two girlfriends, you know who you are, who embraced and prayed with me for revelation over the years. If it were not for "Claire," I might still be struggling.

I give my extended arms in love and gratitude to my children and their spouses who encouraged me to write this book, especially when I was convinced that I could not do it.

My deep appreciation and gratitude goes out to Dr. Willard F. Harley, Jr. who took time out of his busy schedule years ago to bring me direction and hope; and who again took time out of his schedule a second time, some months ago, to encourage me to write this book.

Above all, I thank my God for His Word, on whose authority I stand, that states the truth about sexual fulfillment in marriage.

Introduction

I PASSED FIVE STORES today and scanned the titles of articles in fifteen magazines. Nothing has changed in forty years. All these years I have been checking out magazines for articles on how to increase a woman's sexual libido. I would read a title and get excited, thinking that maybe something in the article would help me and other women. But instead it turned out to be all about how to dress sexily for him, some hot new sex position I should try, the sexiest thing I could do for him on a date, and so on. They all continued on that wavelength; it was all about what to do for him. In my circle of friends and acquaintances, it is not the husband who needs his sexual libido raised—it is the wife!

This book is not about all the different positions you and your husband could try to make sex hotter than ever. There are other good books that illustrate and talk about positions. This is not a book about helping women who have challenges with a husband who is addicted to alcohol, pornography, or drugs and how she can have a better sex life with him. Those issues should be dealt with by a professional counselor. Although reading this book might relieve you of some of your long-held taboos and give you insight that will help you change some negative behaviors, it will not provide you with rules regarding the dos and don'ts of sexual activity.

This book is about how to up your sexual drive (also called libido) for your husband. In my experience, "How do I increase my sexual passion for my husband?" is the question most commonly asked by wives.

Regardless of age, there are three criteria that must be met for a woman to crave sex and keep craving sex with her husband:

1. A woman has to be able to achieve climax/orgasm.
2. A woman has to feel cherished by her husband.
3. A woman has to continue to be attracted to her husband.

These criteria will be discussed in *Silk On Fire*, a guide on how to crave sex, keep your libido high, and experience hot lovemaking.

1

Jade's Story

JADE WAS TWENTY-TWO and was looking forward to her honeymoon. She and her fiancé, Jerry, had read some very explicit but healthy books about sexual fulfillment together and had even discussed them somewhat. She had a healthy relationship with her parents, and she and her mom talked about sex openly.

After a few nights into the honeymoon, Jade realized she was missing something. She was not feeling sexually fulfilled. Was it possible that she was not having a complete orgasm? She didn't really feel she could ask her mother. She lived a great distance from her and didn't feel this was a proper phone subject. She and her husband discussed how she could have more pleasure and tried different things, but it was to no avail. Jerry became disappointed about not being able to fulfill his wife sexually and felt that it was his fault but didn't know what else he could do. Jade didn't want to make him feel any more like a failure by discussing it. This went on for some time, with Jade often crying herself to sleep and wondering whether she would ever feel anything more than this.

After Jade had been married a year, Marcy, a close friend who had gotten married a year before Jade, came to visit her. Jade felt that this was an opportunity. She just had to draw up enough courage to ask Marcy about her sexual experiences in marriage. After all, she and Marcy were close and had talked about a lot of things over the years. Amazingly, it took quite a bit of courage to ask. She asked her friend what it was like to have sexual fulfillment. Was it really as amazing as the books and magazines implied? Did Marcy really feel fireworks and all that cool stuff Jade had read about? Immediately Marcy started to laugh. She changed the subject on Jade and never returned to it again. Jade was mortified and absolutely shocked. She found it difficult to believe that her close girlfriend wouldn't want to talk about the subject in order to help her.

The issue again went on the back burner until Jade finally approached her mother. Although her mother listened well and felt sympathy and compassion for her, she couldn't seem to offer anything more. Her mother told Jade she hoped things would change for her, but that was about all she said. Jade began to wonder if she was one of those women who would never be able to have an orgasm. Maybe she was frigid; maybe she would never be completely sexually satisfied. These thoughts brought on a deep sadness.

Two years into her marriage, Jade finally drummed up enough courage to talk to her doctor about it. He asked her a few good questions and then said he'd be glad to set her and her husband up with a professional sexual therapy clinic in Saskatoon. The workers there had been trained at the famous Masters and Johnson Institute. Jade had heard of them—their success rate was superior—and had also read some articles and books by them. So with great anticipation and hope, Jade and Jerry planned around the appointment, saving up so they could travel the eight hundred miles to the nearest clinic.

Finally the day arrived. A husband-and-wife team interviewed Jade and Jerry together, then separately, and then together again. The therapy team concluded, "Well, there's nothing really wrong with either one of you. You have so much going for you in your marriage. Just enjoy what you have. You have more than a lot of couples have. You both have a wonderful commitment to each other, and we are sure things will get better."

That was all they were going to get from the famous Masters and Johnson clinic? Jade wasn't about to "just enjoy what she had" because she did not have sexual fulfillment! Jade soon became a mom and busied herself with all the tasks mothering entails. Things didn't get better, and Jade's sexual fulfillment went on the back burner again.

Many years later, a woman named Ann came to speak in their community about surviving sexual trauma. Since this woman was comfortable speaking openly about sexual issues, Jade thought, "Finally, I've got someone I can talk to. This woman is speaking on surviving sexual abuse and counsels couples in need of sexual help; I am going to approach her."

But to Jade's dismay, it was another dead end. Ann asked some questions, but when she discovered that there was no sexual trauma in Jade's background, she said, "Well, just continue what you are doing; continue to search for fulfillment."

By this time Jade was becoming extremely discouraged. If she couldn't get help from the top sexual therapists from Masters and Johnson Institute and couldn't get any help from a woman who spoke to women internationally about intimate issues, where could she get help?

Another few years passed. Jade began seeing a female marriage counselor she seemed to connect with. However, after asking the same routine questions, the counselor merely encouraged her to keep doing what she was doing.

Jade turned to prayer. She tried prayer with some girlfriends, but by this time a lot of anger had moved into her relationship. This anger would arise when she and her husband came together sexually. She found herself grinding her teeth because of the anger that had built up inside of her about all the years she had spent serving her husband without any sexual fulfillment for herself.

At about this time, she had an intimate conversation with another girlfriend, Claire. Jade humbled herself again and talked frankly with her girlfriend. She just came out and said, "Actually, Claire, to be completely honest, after all my years of marriage, I don't know if I'm having an orgasm or not. How does a woman know if she is having an orgasm? I have a lot of sexual excitement with my husband during the act, but what does an orgasm actually feel like?"

For the first time in Jade's life, someone actually told her what an orgasm felt like. Claire also asked Jade a question: "After you have had an orgasm or what you think is an orgasm, can you stand to be touched on your clitoris?"

Jade replied, "I think so, yes."

Claire said, "Well I'm pretty sure with every woman, and I know with me, that after climax I can't handle to be touched there."

"Oh...I've never had that sensation. I've never had an experience where it bothered me to be touched on the clitoris." Jade returned home after that conversation, confident that she had never experienced orgasm.

Soon after, Jade and Jerry took a marriage course called "His Needs, Her Needs," and one of the textbooks for that curriculum was authored by Dr. Willard F. Harley Jr. Jade again humbled herself and did a very brave thing—she called Dr. Willard Harley's office to make an appointment with him. He was a marriage counselor as well as an author. On the first ring, Dr. Harley answered. She actually didn't need to make an appointment, as he said he could talk right then. Jade wasn't really ready but seized the moment.

Dr. Harley asked, "How many times a year do you have an orgasm with your husband?"

Embarrassed, Jade colored the truth and took a number out of the air. "Twice a year," she replied.

Then he asked a couple more questions, and she confessed, "You know, Dr. Harley, I don't know if I ever have really had an orgasm."

Without expressing any surprise, he told her, "Well, I can tell you how you can have an orgasm. Have you ever tried using a vibrator?"

Jade tried to hide her shock that the man on the phone was asking her if she had ever had an orgasm using a vibrator. "No, I haven't," she replied.

"Get a vibrator with two speeds, and experiment with both speeds as you use the vibrator on yourself or you and your husband use it. If you practice with it, I guarantee you will have an orgasm," he said.

After a bit more conversation she thanked him and hung up. Jade then began putting together a plan. She realized that having an orgasm was going to take some very strong, focused, disciplined action. She began to believe that she could have one and would have one, so she told her husband, "I am going to have sex with you every night until I have an orgasm."

Jerry blinked and calmly said to her, "No problem. I'd be happy to oblige every night!" After three nights in a row of trying different things, Jade had an orgasm. The two biggest factors that contributed to her success were that somebody had actually explained to her how it felt to have an orgasm and how stimulation of the clitoris would feel afterward, and that Dr. Harley had supported her and explained to her how to successfully have an orgasm.[1]

Jade's story is my story. In this day and age, women should not be struggling like this. Even thirty-nine years ago, I should have been able to get help within my first year of marriage. Masters and Johnson, you really missed this one! Counselors and inspirational speakers say they want to help people sexually. Spiritual counselors pray with people but often don't really know how to ask the right questions. I encourage parents to talk to their daughters and sons openly about sex. Every mother should explain to her daughter how to achieve orgasm. It is my hope that this book helps. I am thankful for my eventual success, but the fact that it took two decades of marriage to have an orgasm is a tragedy. If this guide helps even one woman reach sexual fulfillment, I will be ecstatic.

---

[1] Dr. Willard F. Harley Jr., in discussion with the author, 1998.

2

How Do I Achieve Orgasm?

THE REASON I don't hide this chapter in the middle is because if a woman hasn't been able to climax with her husband, she will not be able to improve her sexual drive. Since this book is about how to *crave* sex with your husband, learning how to achieve orgasm should be first on a wife's list.

If a woman has not *ever* had an orgasm with her husband, not only will her sexual passion not reach its potential, but anger and bitterness will creep in and taint the entire marriage, as it did in Jade's case. Boredom will certainly be part of the intimate act, and as her husband reaches for her to have sex, she will become resentful of him and of his action. Some of you women reading this book will be able to identify. Remaining in this stage—the pre-orgasmic stage—will prevent sexual fulfillment from developing and marital happiness from increasing.

In this chapter I am going to explain three things: what the *phases* of lovemaking are, what an orgasm *feels* like, and how you can *achieve* orgasm.

The Four Phases of Lovemaking
(or The Sexual Response Cycle)

Both men and women go through these phases, which are most often described as:

1. *arousal* or excitement
2. *peaking* or plateau
3. *climax* or orgasm
4. *relaxation* or recovery

There are different names for them, but to keep it simple, I'm going to refer to them as *arousal, peaking, climax,* and *relaxation.*

Diagram 1:
A Woman's Sexual Response Cycle

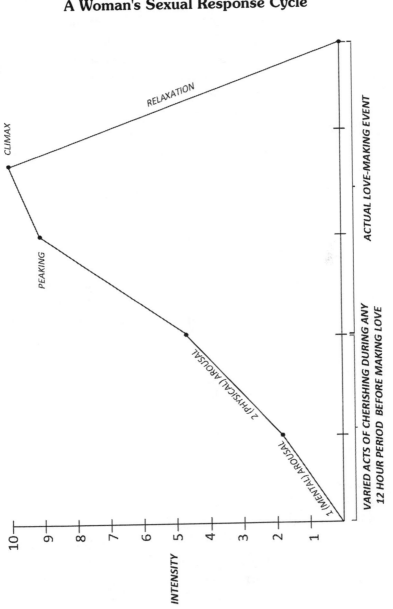

Illustrated by Andrew Willis

As you look at diagram 1, you will be aware of when each phase occurs and approximately how long each one takes in comparison to the other phases. Bear in mind that these will change slightly in duration as you go through different seasons of life and as you age. For instance, a woman in her twenties who has children under foot all day might take longer to get aroused than would a woman in her sixties who has just come home from shopping for lingerie and is kissed by her husband while *he* is preparing supper for the two of them. Even men vary. A man in his twenties will have a very short arousal period of mere seconds while a man in his fifties may experience an arousal period that takes minutes.

AROUSAL

The arousal stage for a woman involves two levels. The first level is the emotion of wanting sex. During this first level of arousal, a woman feels very sexy. She will begin to stop thinking about the day and all its problems, all the kids, her work, the garden, and the house. She will put aside the issues she and her husband argued about an hour ago, as her body is starting to feel sensuous. That's arousal, and that is what she was designed for! At this stage she will begin to want to engage in sexual acts with her husband.

The second level occurs when her partner is fondling her body. During foreplay, most men want to fondle the breasts and crotch area. Most women eventually want this, but only after they've reached the first level of arousal. This is why women often get irritated. A woman's husband may start fondling all his favorite spots before she has become emotionally and sexually aroused. To her, it feels like she is being groped. But when she informs him and he listens and follows instructions as to what she likes, arousal in her body happens, both physically and mentally. At this stage a woman wants to push her body against him; she then wants more of what he is physically arousing in her.

At this point a couple will mutually decide if the woman wants to reach climax through digital stimulation (hand to clitoris) or coitus (penis inside vagina). If the woman wants to climax through coitus, then as her husband penetrates her with his erect penis, she needs to do a combination of three things:

1. She should contract her pubococcygeus (PCG) muscle, which tightens the vagina on the inserted penis.
2. She should thrust her pelvis rapidly.
3. She should assume a position that increases pressure on the clitoris and resistance to the penis in the vaginal opening.

If the woman wants to climax with clitoral stimulation, then her husband should continue clitoral stimulation with his hand or a vibrator until she peaks.

PEAKING

At this stage women are going beyond arousal and are beginning to feel like this is what they have been missing. Eventually a woman will feel a flush of warmth and tingling. This profound intense feeling is concentrated in the pelvic area. Sometimes she will feel like she is going to lose control. If she truly wants to climax, she has to decide to let her body take over. She must tell herself, "This is going to be good." As she allows herself to lose control, she will experience an orgasm. Once a woman gets more confident about reaching a climax, she can learn to control the peaking and make it last longer before climax thus creating a more powerful climax.

CLIMAX

As a woman lets herself go emotionally, her clitoris and vagina will contract. Heat and feelings of euphoria will wash over her body, and this will last anywhere from two to six seconds or longer.

RELAXATION

The final stage brings a feeling of total relaxation as the body begins to cool down. Different books offer different explanations about this phase. Some say that women like to cuddle and talk to their husbands after climaxing, while others say that women, like men, want to just lie there, not move, and go to sleep because of the incredible, delicious sedative that they have received. Women should choose the scenario that they like best, as both reactions are totally normal. It may have to do with personality, where they are in their marriage, how tired they are, or whether they need something else emotionally, but whatever it is, it doesn't matter. Women should do whatever they like to do during this phase. They should allow themselves to go into a beautiful relaxation mode. They should tell their husbands what they like to do during this period; if they are extremely different from their husbands, they can agree on a compromise and proceed with mutual agreement.

Some people will say that there is no way that a woman wants to have intercourse with her husband after her climax. They claim that when she's done, she just wants to go to sleep. The same is often true of men after they climax; they will take some time to become aroused again and therefore are not motivated to bring their wives to climax. The solution is for both partners to figure it out so that they both have pleasure and fulfillment. A good suggestion is to mix it up. A couple might find that during intercourse the wife doesn't climax, though it arouses her to have her husband use digital stimulation on her after he climaxes. At other times she may like to be stimulated to climax first and then have her husband enter her for his climax during intercourse. Women shouldn't be afraid to try lovemaking in many different ways.

WHAT AN ORGASM FEELS LIKE

It is confusing when your friends or magazines or books say, "When you have an orgasm, you will know it." If you're *pre-orgasmic* (haven't had an orgasm yet), you don't know what that means. Of course, *after* you have had an orgasm, it makes sense. When you have an orgasm, you really know it. But before you have an orgasm, you don't know what people are talking about and you keep asking yourself, "Is this it?"

I'm going to refer to the above phases now as I tell you exactly what an orgasm feels like. I will explain to you what each phase feels like to most women. Some people might use different words, but I'll try to keep things simple.

AROUSAL Presuming that you have made it to the second level of arousal and you are receiving proper stimulation, there will be a fluctuation of sensation. You may even ask, "Did I feel something?" It is like a flutter. You may feel a flush of warmth, some tingling, or waves of euphoric feelings sweep over you. There will be a tingling—almost a buzz—starting in the genital area. At this time you can control the sensation, and with your mind you could stop it, but don't!

PEAKING Here's the key: you have to decide right here, right now whether you want to lose control. (Trust me, at this moment you want to lose control; you don't want to analyze it.)

As you "push" into this fluttering sensation and give yourself permission to let yourself go, the fluttering will become stronger. Then you will feel a building sensation, and as you think, "It's coming, it's coming," you will give in to this explosive sensation.

When you get good at climaxing, you will be able to control the sensation, stopping and starting it for a limited time in order to have a more powerful orgasm.

CLIMAX If there is nothing penetrating your vagina when this explosive sensation takes over your body, you're going to have a stronger and more intense climax because there is nothing inside the vagina for those contractions to hit. It will actually feel like the muscle of the inside of the vagina is making a bigger contraction, and for most women, this feels better than a climax through coitus. (But again, I'm not making the rules; I'm just explaining to you why a woman often has a better climax before or after intercourse.) When your husband's penis is inside you, although the orgasm may not feel as powerful, you will feel the desire to push against the penis with your body. However, once the orgasm is fully upon you, your body will take over. It's an intense feeling all over the pelvic area, and at that moment it's all about you. You won't be able to even think about caressing your husband or doing anything for him. This is about you, as it should be.

You will feel an inner explosion of beautiful contractions inside the pelvic area that will be like nothing you've ever felt before. It's like being on a ride at a fair; you know when you go up and then you drop and feel like you left your stomach behind? Well, that is what it feels like, but it's way better. It is so powerful that you may feel like yelling or screaming (and you should let yourself go and yell) during the actual orgasm. It truly is amazing!

RELAXATION After the orgasm has ended, you will not want to have your clitoris directly touched for a few minutes. At this point you will move your husband's hand away or move the vibrator, as the area is just too sensitive. This is also a good test for yourself if you ever want to know if you have had an orgasm or not.

HOW DO I ACHIEVE ORGASM?

"How do I achieve this amazing orgasm?" you ask. I am so glad you asked this question. If you have decided you are going to have an orgasm, you will.

Unless you have had surgery that removed the clitoris, you are going to have an orgasm using the following technique. Keep in mind that it's going to take belief, patience, and focus. You must make a decision to practice this technique every night, rain or shine, tired or not, until you have an orgasm. Be encouraged! Your husband will love this adventure that you are taking him on. Enjoy the journey, and of course engage in all other kinds of sexual activity that you and your husband both enjoy.

The clitoris *absolutely* needs to be stimulated. There are some women whose clitoris is more connected physically to their vagina and who can have orgasms by just intercourse. But the easiest way for a woman to have an orgasm is by clitoral stimulation, which means direct contact with a hand or vibrator.

We know that after childbirth the vaginal muscle walls will not be as responsive as before[2] (see Pubococcygeus Muscle) but other than this, I don't know why some women cannot experience vaginal orgasm. Perhaps it has to do with anatomy, as everyone's can be slightly different. The clitoris might have more nerve endings connecting to the vaginal wall in some women. But I don't spend a lot of time thinking about it. The important issue is to first, train yourself to have an orgasm digitally, then, after you have been sexually fulfilled, if you like, you can spend more time training yourself to have one during actual intercourse.

The following diagram shows clearly where the female organs are. Women should all know exactly where and what their female parts are and how they work so they can achieve orgasm.

---

2 Lori and Paul Byerly, "The Female Genitals," The Marriage Bed, accessed May 11, 2013, http://site.themarriagebed.com/biology/her-plumbing.

Today more help and illustrations are available in this area than ever before. It amazes me how so many young people haven't even looked at a medical illustration of women's genitalia. Some women have looked at detailed diagrams but have not been educated about the anatomy. Now is the time to be fully educated, so do look at the diagram.

Diagram 2: External Female Sex Organs

Female External Sex Organs:

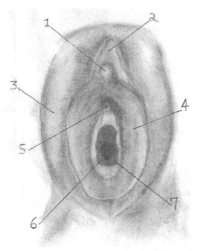

Illustrated by Debra Mundy

1. Clitoris
2. Clitoral Hood (prepuce)
3. Labia Majora (outer lips)
4. Labia Minora (inner lips)
5. Urethral opening
6. Vaginal opening
7. Hymen

Description and Function of the Female Sex Organs

The Vulva: "Vulva" is the name applied to the external female genitals as a whole. As a woman becomes aroused, the entire vulva becomes engorged with blood, resulting in swelling and darkening of the external genitals. The swollen tissue is much like a water bed in that touching any place causes ripples of sensation throughout the whole area. For this reason it is possible for a woman to have an orgasm without the clitoris being directly stimulated.

The Mons Veneris: This term refers to a pad of fat that covers the pubic bone. Pressure on the mons can be pleasurable due to the presence of nerve endings. The mons is covered with pubic hair. During intercourse, the mons serves as a shock absorber between the pubic bones of the man and the woman.

The Labia Majora: Also called the large or outer lips, the labia majora start at the thigh and extend inward, surrounding the rest of the vulva. The outer edges are covered with hair, and the inner edges are smooth. The skin of the outer lips is rich in blood vessels and darker than the skin of the thighs. During arousal the labia majora swell and become even darker. Prior to adolescence the outer lips come together, covering the rest of the vulva; after puberty the lips part slightly, showing some of the labia minora.

The **Labia Minora:** Also called the smaller or inner lips, the labia minora are located between the labia majora. They meet at the bottom below the entrance to the vagina and join at the top with the clitoral hood. The smaller lips are hairless, smooth, and irregular. They usually protrude beyond the labia majora, and one is larger than the other. The small lips contain many blood vessels and nerve endings along with sweat and oil glands. Any movement of these lips pulls on the clitoral hood, causing stimulation. The labia minora darken progressively during arousal, becoming darkest just before climax. Women who have been pregnant have darker inner lips than those who have not.

The Urethral Opening: The opening of the urethra is located above the vagina. Very active sex, especially after a time of abstinence, can bruise the urethra. Intercourse can also force bacteria up into the urethra, leading to an infection. Urinating after intercourse and gradually working up to greater levels of activity can prevent these problems.

The Clitoris: The clitoris is often described as a small penis, though the analogy leads to some misconceptions. The glans (head) of the clitoris has more nerve endings than the glans of the penis, and these nerve endings are packed into a much smaller area. In fact, the clitoris is so sensitive that some women dislike direct contact. The clitoris swells slightly during arousal and then retracts under the clitoral hood as arousal continues and the clitoris becomes hypersensitive. Husbands sometimes misinterpret the "disappearing clitoris" as a sign of diminishing arousal, but it is the exact opposite. The shaft of the clitoris runs up under the hood and then splits into two parts known as the crura. The crura run back down under the labia majora, and attach to the lower pubic bone.

The Clitoral Hood: The hood covers the clitoris, protecting it from excessive stimulation and stimulating the clitoris as it slides over it. Men sometimes think they need to retract the hood to get to the clitoris when manually or orally stimulating their wife, but this is unnecessary at best and can result in overstimulation that borders on pain. Dried secretions known as smegma can collect under the hood, causing pain during sex. Retracting the hood when washing can prevent this problem. (Most medical professionals recommend using water only to wash the vulva.)

The Vagina: The vagina has been described as a potential space, as it is a collapsed tube most of the time. In the unaroused state, the vagina is three to four and a half inches long. The walls of the vagina are composed of three layers—a mucous membrane (outer layer), muscle (middle layer), and fibrous tissue (inner layer). The outer layer is full of folds that are similar to, but softer than, the folds in the roof of the mouth. This texturing provides the man with the friction he needs to climax during intercourse. The middle layer, which is mostly in the outer third of the vagina, contracts during arousal, firmly gripping the penis during intercourse. The fibrous inner layer provides structural support. All three layers of the vagina have an abundance of blood vessels but very few nerve endings. In fact, the inner two-thirds of the vagina are usually incapable of discerning touch.

The walls of the vagina continually produce secretions that moisten and clean the vagina. During sexual arousal (within ten to thirty seconds of the start of stimulation), the walls of the vagina sweat a slippery fluid that serves as a lubricant. Because the lubricant is subject to gravity, it may not readily reach the entrance of the vagina if the woman is lying down. The quantity and thickness of the fluid varies from woman to woman and changes considerably during a woman's cycle. As arousal continues, two things happen to lengthen the vagina: the swelling of the labia majora pushes the entrance of the vagina outward, and the back of the vagina extends past the cervix into the body. The lower third of the vagina closes down, and the upper two-thirds opens up.

The Hymen: Just inside the opening of the vagina is the hymen, a fold of tissue that usually covers part of the vagina. In extreme cases the hymen covers the entire vagina and must be broken to allow menstruation. Although it was once thought that the hymen was rather delicate, it has recently been learned that the hymen is actually very elastic and capable of healing quickly. A woman who had intercourse only a few times in the past may have a normal-looking hymen. Because the hymen normally covers only part of the vagina, it is very possible for a woman to use tampons for years and still have an intact hymen. The hymen is a poor indicator of virginity, since a nonvirgin can have a hymen and a virgin can have no trace of a hymen because she never had much of one or because some activity has destroyed it. Despite horror stories about the pain and bleeding that accompany intercourse for the first time, most woman experience only minor discomfort and minimal bleeding. In very rare cases, the hymen is so tough that intercourse can't occur until a gynecologist aids in breaking it. A premarital exam or a bit of self-exploration can help you avoid wedding night problems.

The Bartholin's Glands: Once wrongly thought to be the source of vaginal lubrication, the Bartholin's glands actually only secrete a few drops of fluid when the woman is about to orgasm. It is believed these glands are designed to make the normally acidic vagina more alkaline and thus more receptive to sperm.

The Pubococcygeus Muscle: Also called the PC muscle, it surrounds the vagina, the urethra, and the anus. The PC muscle experiences involuntary rhythmic contractions during orgasm but can also be squeezed voluntarily. It has been found that the stronger this muscle is, the more easily and intensely women can orgasm. PC muscle strength is particularly necessary for coital orgasm, and women who have a weak PC muscle are incapable of experiencing orgasm during intercourse. Kegel exercises can be done to strengthen this muscle.

The G-Spot: Located two to three inches inside the vagina on the top or roof, this area produces distinct feelings and often swells when stimulated. The G-spot is named after Earnest Grafenberg, who first noted the erotic sensitivity of this location in the '50s. However, the existence of glandular structures in this area was first noted by Dr. Skene in 1880, and medical mention of the area goes back to ancient Rome.

A great deal of debate centers around what it is and what it does, but it's fairly clear the G-spot does exist. A husband can locate the G-spot by inserting one or two fingers nearly as far as possible into the aroused vagina while the woman lies on her stomach. If the husband keeps his hand palm down and gently wiggles his fingers in a "come here" motion, he will stimulate the spot. The first reaction of most women to this stimulation is getting a strong feeling of needing to urinate, but this passes, and the sensation becomes arousing. Continued stimulation usually causes the area to swell, making it easier to locate.

Some women are able to orgasm from G-spot stimulation alone, while others greatly enjoy the so-called "blended orgasm," which results from a combination of clitoral and G-spot stimulation. The G-spot can also be stimulated during intercourse, particularly in rear entry positions; this may explain why some women experience powerful orgasm in these positions. Some scientists believe the G-spot is composed of the same tissue that becomes the prostate in men and may be the cause of female ejaculation.

The Cervix: Often thought of as being at the end of the vagina, the cervix is actually on the top or roof of the vagina. During intercourse, the penis slides under and past the cervix. Recent research has determined that the cervix has a good number of nerve cells that are much more sensitive when the woman's blood estrogen level is high (near ovulation). This explains why a pap smear sometimes hurts and sometimes doesn't. It may also be part of the reason that some women find coital orgasm easier at certain times of the month.[3]

The clitoris has to be directly stimulated either by your hand, by your spouse's hand, by oral sex, or by a vibrator. I will take the time to explain each one. Something that is very necessary is lubricant. If you are using the technique of oral sex (the man's tongue licking the woman's clitoris), the lubricant is built in. The husband can also use his saliva on his fingers or his wife's saliva if stimulating his wife's clitoris by hand. A man's saliva is the best natural lubricant there is. Women's genital fluids are made up of the same chemical solutions as their saliva. Some women have never tried their husband's saliva as a lubricant, let alone oral sex, as they are extremely bashful to try this, but I encourage you to try both the lubricants you buy in a drugstore and saliva.

Some women have never used lubricant because they have never needed it. As they age and need extra lubricant applied, they are too embarrassed to ask anyone about it because it is such a new phenomenon to them in their middle age or senior years.

Then there are women who use lubricant but only to enable the penis to penetrate the vagina without irritation. These women have never used it on their clitoris for an orgasm. I encourage

---

3 Ibid

all women to use it liberally to experience orgasm for the first time. Many women use it all the time!

If you are using lubricant other than natural saliva, be sure that it is a proper lubricant you buy at a pharmacy. You will find lubricant in the condom aisle. For some women, it is embarrassing to buy intimate products, but it's something they just have to do. An option for them is to buy lubricant in big centers where people don't know them or get a friend or husband to buy it. I recommend Astroglide, but you should feel free to try them all. Some are more natural than others. Some come paraben-free. You will find one you like more than others.

The other important factor is for your husband to have clean, short, smooth nails. If your husband chews his fingernails, he will have jagged edges. Sharp, jagged fingernails are nasty when they come in contact with sensitive parts, so before you begin this exercise, tell him in a very cute and sexy tone that you are going to give him a manicure that he will enjoy. If his nails need to be clipped, so be it. Always finish up with an emery board so they are completely smooth. Cuddle up to him and do it in bed. He will love the attention, and you will benefit from getting his fingernails smooth.

Of course, whether you want to try this by yourself through masturbation or with your husband doesn't matter; do whatever makes you feel comfortable. The most important thing is to start taking steps to ensure that you are sexually pleasured.

If you are a pre-orgasmic woman, you might prefer masturbation alone to get your body to respond to climaxing. There is absolutely nothing wrong with choosing to masturbate. At the beginning, it can take away the pressure of feeling like you are performing for your husband. If you are alone, you can take the time to fantasize about your husband without anxiety or feeling the pressure of an expectation.

If you become successful at climaxing with masturbation, you can share with your husband what you have discovered. You can tell him what feels good and whether you want him to use his hand, vibrator, or lubricant. Trust that he will be all for whatever you suggest.

In the past masturbation has been a taboo issue. It came up a lot in religious books years ago. If you feel there's something wrong with masturbation, you need to prove it to yourself and not just believe some past myth you were told. I actually don't mind saying that I use the Bible as my foundation on what is right or wrong. I have never found *anywhere* in the Bible where it states or even insinuates that masturbation is wrong.

I want to release anyone who may have a misconception about masturbation. Masturbation is a wonderful way for a woman to discover how she can be sexually pleasured. If you are very shy (and if up to this time you have not been talking very much about the art of lovemaking with your husband), you might want to try masturbating to reach your first orgasm so that you can talk it out better later with your husband when you have more confidence.

If you are planning to practice by yourself, plan on having the house to yourself or at least being in the privacy of your bedroom with the door locked. The best plan if you are not shy is to tell your husband what you are attempting to do and ask him to help you keep the kids away from the bedroom or give you an hour or two alone in the house. If he is not available to do this, and you have small children, consider setting up a time to have your children cared for in somebody else's home. Tell your friend you'll return the favor. There's no need to disclose *what* you are doing; just say you need a couple of hours to yourself.

Play some music in the background. Beware that some music can be very annoying. Some music is set too fast, and sometimes a woman doesn't want singing; instead, she just might want something very subtle in the background. You pick, as it's your afternoon. The important issue is to get the right ambiance in the room so that nothing is annoying, including music, temperature, and light.

It also is really nice to put your jar of lubricant in a bowl of hot water. Once you get that warmed up, lie on your bed with a towel underneath you so you won't worry about getting lubricant on the bed linen. Put lots of pillows behind your head. Get comfortable. Once your privacy is ensured, the phone is turned off, the room is warm, a towel is underneath you, you are naked from at least the waist down, the music of your choice is playing softly in the background (or not), and lubricant and a vibrator are beside you, you are ready.

That is correct—I did say vibrator. There are many kinds. Please believe me when I say it has to give a strong vibration. Purchase one with a large head, not a tiny tip. (check out the Hitachi Wand as well as others.) The larger head will cover more of the area getting stimulated. Only buy vibrators with two or more speeds. Try each speed; one of them will give you the vibration you need for an orgasm. Getting a vibrator is not that difficult these days. If you can walk into one of the sex stores, do it. And it is always more fun when your husband is with you. Many people don't like to go into stores that have sex toys on display. I completely understand; sex is a very intimate part of life, as it should be. Some women and men feel that their intimate lives are on display just by walking in. In the privacy of your home a person can check out online boutiques that carry many sex toys and vibrators.

Give yourself permission to manually stimulate your clitoris with a vibrator or with your own hand. Use lots of lubrication on the clitoris and genital area, and do whatever is sexy for you. The clitoris needs to be well lubricated. Some women have natural lubrication, especially when they're young. When you are sexually aroused, a natural lubricant in the vaginal area will be secreted around the clitoris, but for guaranteed success it is recommended that you have all the tools that you might need handy. Apply the lubricant liberally all around the genital area or wherever it feels good. The clitoris itself needs lubricant. I repeat this because lubricant is the key.

Proceed with this exercise for at least thirty minutes. Go as long as you want. If you are masturbating without your husband nearby, you won't have the pressure of feeling that you're asking your husband to go too long, which basically is a script in your head that you need to replace.

Using short strokes in a circular or up-and-down motion, keep your hand in contact with the clitoris and concentrate on what feels comfortable. Just relax and get to know your body and its responses. After a few minutes, begin using the vibrator.

If you haven't used a vibrator before, you might find that using it directly against your skin is too intense the first few times, so try using the vibrator with your underwear on or a piece of thin material between you and the vibrator. Try one speed for awhile before trying the other. Then go back and forth until you have found what feels the best.

Continue to add lubricant liberally to prevent any irritating friction. Put warm lubricant on your fingers and on your genital area. Use the diagram if you need to really find your clitoris. You will need to have lots of lubricant on the clitoris so that there is no friction between your fingers and the hood of the clitoris. You may want to stimulate the clitoris after you go around the labia of the vagina. Again, it's your body. Do what you want, but keep in mind that the clitoris will need to be stimulated eventually in order for you to have the orgasm, as orgasms can only happen when the clitoris is stimulated directly or indirectly. If you are pre-orgasmic, go with immediately trying to stimulate the clitoris. Begin moving your hand in a circular motion. Do it lightly before intensifying the pressure. You want it to feel really good. Eventually you should feel a type of warmth, fullness, and tingling inside the vulva area. It is difficult to define the actual spot.

A technique that really works is to add your own voice to the exercise. Speak quietly to yourself with confidence. Use phrases like:

- This feels so good.
- I am going to have an orgasm.
- I am capable of having an orgasm.
- My body is going to respond sexually.

- I have a beautiful body.
- No wonder my husband loves touching my clitoris.
- I am so sexy.
- Imagine him looking at me right now.
- He would be getting so excited right now.
- His penis would be hardening and getting big.

When you begin to feel a warm sensation, continue stimulating yourself with the same rhythm. *Do not stop*. It is important to continue the stimulation if you are to reach orgasm. The sensation of warmth and tingling that floods the pelvis and sometimes other parts of the body is an indication that you are at the point just before actual orgasm. Many women who experience it think this is the complete orgasm and mistakenly discontinue stimulation at this point. If you stop the stimulation, even though you already feel the warmth or the contractions, the orgasm may stop. If you continue the same stimulation beyond this stage, you will go on to feel the actual orgasm.

As you become more sexually aroused, start making noises like ooh and aah in different cadences. You will begin to peak at a point where you've never peaked before. As you are making the noises and enjoying the feeling, you make a decision: "I'm giving into this. I'm going to allow myself to lose control." When the climax comes, you're going to feel it like nothing you've ever felt before. It feels like there's a vibration going on in the genital area that spreads into the entire pelvic area. It will grab you like a huge convulsion. The feeling is amazing. You will have an orgasm, and if you are not successful the first night, do it again on the second night, the third night, the fourth night, and on as many nights as it takes until you get it right. You will have an orgasm if you keep practicing.

There is absolutely nothing wrong with choosing to masturbate so that you can check your body's sensations without the pressure of succeeding or failing with your husband. If you practice with your husband and don't achieve orgasm the first time, your husband might feel that he has failed. This, in turn, will be picked up by you, and you might wrongly believe it is your fault for "making him" feel like a loser. Nobody needs these negative feelings.

On the other hand, there is something to be said for navigating this new experience with your husband and having your husband help you achieve orgasm for the first time. What you will lose when you do the masturbating is the excitement of having the sexual experience with your husband. If you haven't masturbated before, on your first attempt you might feel like it is not going anywhere. This is totally understandable, as you are not used to getting excited without your husband. This is the plus side of having your husband help you reach your first orgasm instead of masturbating by yourself.

So if your husband is beside you (it's wonderful to have his arm underneath your head and his other hand touching your clitoris, but sometimes he might like to be on his knees while stimulating your clitoris), soft music of your choice is playing, the room is at the temperature you want, and a bottle of warm lubricant is handy, you are ready to begin.

A man gets very excited upon seeing his wife's genitals becoming aroused. I know a lot of women are embarrassed by this; that's why they have a lights-out policy during lovemaking. They just can't believe their husbands want to look at their nakedness, let alone their exposed genitals. But I want to strongly emphasize that a man gets *very excited* when looking at his woman's nakedness all over. You can help use this to your advantage.

This is an exercise in which you are pampering yourself so you can have an orgasm. When you begin you may not have entered into the arousal stage, as you may be just treating it as an exercise. That's OK. Begin where you begin. You may not be excited yet for your husband, but as he reaches down and starts to stimulate you, begin to fantasize. Begin to imagine your husband getting sexually excited for you, because he will be, and most women do like it when their husbands are sexually aroused by them.

As your husband arouses you by stimulating your clitoris with lots of lubricant, relax. Let him look at you and get excited. Give him the freedom to talk about how he is excited about seeing you and seeing your naked beauty. Be sure that you are comfortable with whatever words he is using. At this point it would be really good for you to talk about how you are feeling aroused. Tell him it feels good, and then move on to instructing him on what to do with his hand. Use pet names or the real name for your genitals—whichever is sexier to you. Don't forget to keep adding lubricant. There is no rule as to what is too much lubricant. Remember that it's all about you. If you begin to feel like his hand is too heavy, just say, "I prefer you to go lighter." If you feel it start to get irritating, put more lubricant on. Don't worry about it running down between your legs and going onto the towel. This is sex at its highest form, and you should not worry about all that other stuff.

As your husband stimulates your clitoris and you begin to feel aroused, you will either want him to apply a little more pressure or you will push up against his hand. I believe that you should probably set a timer for this foreplay. Setting a timer may help, as sometimes women feel that they are taking too long to orgasm. There are these thoughts that keep playing in their heads: "Is he bored? Maybe I should stop; I'm taking too much time." Don't think like that. Your husband is *definitely* not bored. He has a live, willing, warm woman under his hand looking for excitement. He is drinking in your nakedness in all its beauty and becoming aroused.

However, to ensure that you can relax about this, set a very quiet timer to go off in ten to twenty minutes. This will force you to relax and not be thinking, "We are spending too much time on me." Set the timer, and forget about time. When the timer goes off, give yourself permission to continue or not to continue. In other words, you might want to stop the stimulation on your clitoris, continue with lovemaking, and let your husband have an orgasm. The next night start the timer again, but this time set it for two minutes longer.

Some timers make a noticeable tick-tick-tick sound, so you may want to use a timer on a watch or something that does not making an annoying sound. When you try again the next night, you can either set the timer for two minutes longer or tell your husband to pay attention to the clock and let you know when twenty minutes have passed.

What's important is that you relax and are not worried about the length of time this exercise is taking. Do whatever it takes to relax, and allow you husband to stimulate you in this manner for at least ten minutes the first time you try this exercise, eventually building up to twenty minutes or longer.

It is possible that at this point you're not feeling anything or you are feeling frustrated. If this is the case, try turning over on your stomach and having your husband manually stimulate you with his hand underneath you. His hand should go between your legs, underneath your pelvic area. When he puts his well-lubricated hand on your clitoris, you will feel a little different because you now have more control. Your husband's hand is under you. You are on top and can put pressure on his fingers. The whole hand may be too much until you are aroused and want more pressure. One finger is often too pointy, so usually two fingers that are kept together as they rub your clitoris feels best. Here is when you will be glad that you gave him a manicure.

With his hand underneath you, you can push yourself up with your knees or your elbows and maneuver your body so that you can feel the stimulation and pressure on your genitals exactly where you want it. As you become increasingly aroused, you're going to experience a really sensuous feeling that you've never felt before. It's a wonderful sensation that feels a bit like losing control.

If you are a very choleric, bossy woman, this is the point when you are going to have to make a pivotal decision for yourself. If you are a person who likes to be in control and you don't want to let your husband actually know that you are losing control (women who identify with this will know what I am speaking about), you need to ask yourself whether you truly want an orgasm or not. If you do, you have to let yourself lose control.

Push into that feeling emotionally and physically. I suggest you start making noises like ooohhing, ahh ahh-ahh. It can be anything, as women can make themselves become uninhibited emotionally and sexually just by letting their feelings transform into sounds. Making such sounds will accomplish two things: it will do something mentally to you and allow you to physically feel more. Everything is connected at this point—the mind, the emotions, the physique. Although it is the genital area that is being stimulated, all areas are affected.

When you start making noise, it will absolutely push the pedal to the metal for your husband. It will excite him and totally charge him. My husband says it's like having his foot on the pedal of a Ferrari with a powerful V12 motor. This will be a top-notch experience for your husband. It will make him feel very macho and successful as a lover. By being able to arouse you to the point that you are actually excited and making noise, he will feel that you have affirmed his lovemaking ability. And here my point is made: when a woman approaches lovemaking with an attitude of "it's all about me," she creates a hot and sexy experience for both man and woman.

As you make noises and reach a point you've never reached before, you make a decision to give into the feeling and to allow yourself to lose control. The climax will come, and it will be like nothing you've ever felt before. It will feel like there's a convulsion happening in the vaginal/pelvic area, and there is.

It is really important that you practice this either by yourself or with your husband on a regular basis. Your husband is going to love it if you come to him and say, "I want to have sex every night until I have an orgasm." If you are too embarrassed, you should try masturbating.

If you feel comfortable enough telling your husband what you are doing, this is a bonus, as he will be your biggest support. He is going to love the fact that you are actually practicing getting hot and sexy for him. You don't have to say that you're going to try to have an orgasm. Instead, you can say, "I really want to concentrate on my femininity. I want to concentrate on being hot and sexy for you tonight. Would there be time today, tomorrow, or one day this week when you could take the children for a couple of hours?" Believe me, he will move heaven and Earth to do it. (And if he doesn't, keep in mind that I do passion coaching. I am available to help women communicate with their husbands about these issues.)

That's how you have an orgasm. If you are not successful the first night, keep trying. You will have an orgasm if you keep practicing and doing exactly what I have said.

Although this may appear to you to be just about *you*, remember that focusing on you and having a successful orgasm will bring success to both you and your husband. Don't take on an attitude of defeatism, give in to anxiety and fear, and say, "Oh, we won't worry about me tonight, dear." This attitude will not bring results. Change your attitude; change your results. By moving yourself forward in terms of your sexual success, you will ultimately move your marriage forward.

Passion is built on sexual success. Sexual success involves achieving orgasm. In order to even discuss building your sexual passion, you have to learn to achieve orgasm with your husband. I would never tell you that when you and your husband make love, you should just settle for making it a beautiful thing *for him*. Unless a clinical doctor explains to you that you physically cannot have an orgasm because of the way you were born or because of some surgery, you should never accept settling for that. I am very passionate about this subject. If you learn to climax with your husband, you will be on the road to upping your sexual drive and craving sex with your husband.

3

Your Orgasm Is More Important to Your Husband Than...

Your orgasm is more important to your husband than his orgasm. You may think that this is a totally insane statement, but once men learn to pleasure their wives, they usually want to do it more and more. Why? There is nothing more exciting to them as lovers than to see their wives become excited. This is the pinnacle of their sexual experience.

This is why you hear some men justifying why they went to a prostitute—the prostitutes that they pay for display excitement (though it's known that they fake it many, many times). No man wants an unresponsive woman to make love to. No man wants to try to bring his wife to orgasm and then feel that he has failed. It's just not as exciting, and he feels like less of a man. I never, ever encourage women to fake an orgasm. Instead, I want them to have the real thing. As they allow themselves to be heard and seen having their orgasms, they will be fulfilling the needs of themselves and their husbands.

You can be sure that men want to have orgasms as well, but I would take a guess that eight out of ten men would prefer bringing their wives to orgasm and seeing them get excited to having their own orgasm while their wives feel nothing.

In some cultures, it was historically the man's duty to pleasure his wife. He was secondary. I like that, but a woman must be very clear about what she wants. Often a husband will have a false philosophy of "If I have more sex with my wife, I will automatically be a better lover." This is not true. Women must step up to the plate and inform their husbands about what does make them dizzy with excitement.

Oftentimes men will forget what it was they did a few days earlier that pleasured their wives so much. And sometimes women also forget what it was that made the lovemaking so great. Therefore, it's really good for women to share what was a successful lovemaking time for them and why. This keeps the men informed. They will then feel less clumsy and more successful. When they feel successful, they will be more inclined to listen, to do what their wives are telling them, and to believe that they can be all that their women need. This increases the rate of success and fulfillment for both partners. If couples would keep track of their sex life "recipes" like they do with their recipes for food they serve on the table, they would have a more yummy sex life.

Women need to feel released to concentrate on their sexual fulfillment in the relationship. They should not feel that this is selfish. If a man's wife is sexually fulfilled with him, the man is ecstatic and fulfilled, as well.

4

The Importance of Feeling Cherished

"CHERISHING" IS AN old-fashioned word, but I don't think there's any new word that does a better job of describing what a woman needs. The word "cherish" comes from the Old French and Latin languages. The *World Book Dictionary* gives three meanings:[4]

> **Cherish:**
> - to treat with tenderness
> - to keep in the mind
> - to guard carefully

A man who looks after his car or his truck by babying it, keeping it clean, and looking after the motor is cherishing that truck. Think about a man who looks after his bank account and is

---

[4] *World Book Dictionary*, 1986 ed., s.v. "cherish."

very careful as to how much he spends, keeping track of where it goes and of the different accounts that he has. Some men spend a lot of time on their bookkeeping. They cherish the organization of these accounts. Most people have seen homes with special mementos or paintings that are covered in glass to keep the dust away and are highlighted from above or within with special lights. These things are cherished by the people who own them.

I don't want to compare a woman to a thing, money, or a truck, but it's a good way to get an idea of what I am talking about when I say a man cherishes a woman. When he's dating her he finds endless ways to attract her. He finds out what she likes and then usually does it. He phones her, texts her, checks in on her, sends her gifts, and takes her out for a special meal or to entertainment that she likes.

This is consistently true about any man who wants to attract a woman, whether he's got good intentions or bad intentions. He could be a suave charmer who will hurt women in the end or a very charming gentleman who genuinely wants to attract a woman and treat her well. Either way the object is to treat her with a tenderness that will attract and reel her in. I use the phrase "reel her in" because that is what people do. If a man wants someone, he will do his best to attract the person and have the person admire him.

As soon as a woman feels valued and treated with respect and tenderness, she is feeling cherished. A woman doesn't "fall in love" by accident. There has to be some action that contributes to why a woman feels valued. Hearing words of endearment, being on the receiving end of acts of kindness, having a partner with good listening skills, having a partner who gives her lots of gifts or spends a lot of money on her, and having a partner who is available to spend time with her can all contribute to the woman's feeling that she is valued. Once she feels this way, the woman will become enamored of and connected emotionally with the man.

This will lead to the belief that she is "in love" with him. At this point she is vulnerable to being reeled in by the man and to saying yes to one or all of the next steps in their relationship:

1. Sexual intercourse with him
2. Living with him
3. Marriage with him

Notice that I said vulnerable. I am not saying absolutely that she will take the next step, but she is vulnerable to the next step because she has felt cherished.

People don't really analyze this part of it. They think they got married because they fell in love. But they didn't fall "in love"; what really happened was that they became attracted to someone who valued them. This reeled them in; it was infatuation.

Yes, most women were physically attracted to their husbands, but it wasn't until the men actually valued them that the women started having tender feelings and began looking forward to seeing him, listening to him on the phone, waiting for his text message, and waiting for his next visit. As the men continued to court the women or responded in ways that showed respect, they gave the women a feeling of being special and cherished. When this is built up enough over a long enough period of time, it becomes a strong emotional attachment that most refer to as "falling in love." It can lead to men and women truly getting to know each other and feeling like they want to love each other for the rest of their lives, but at the pre-commitment level, my opinion is that it still is infatuation. True love is when the commitment is tested.

The sad or ironic thing is that most men actually think that once they are married or living together, they no longer have to work to make the women feel cherished. In other words, to them, the "dating thing" is over. Women presume that the "dating thing" is what men do naturally. They assume the men they are with will continue to be tender, affectionate in public, generous with their time, and attentive in conversation.

At this point I want to be clear that I am not trying to disrespect men or throw them under the bus. I believe that men who care about their wives truly do not realize that they have disengaged from the very emotional connection that their women need. They honestly are coming from the only mind-set they have about sex, which is based on their male emotions, just as women come from the only mind-set they have, which is based on their female emotions. Innocently, men think their women believe the same thing that they do, which is, "We have each other, and now we can have sex whenever we want it."

What people don't realize is that the act of cherishing is the motor that drives a woman to desire the man sexually in the first place. That is how he made her vulnerable enough to be willing to take the next sexual step. That is how he won her sexually. It is a major mistake that husbands make when they think that they can shut off the very thing that drives women's motors to have sex just because they are having a sexual relationship now.

I have appreciated Dr. Willard Harley's articles on his website, http://www.marriagebuilders.com. The following quote confirms what I believe to be true:

> Receiving the sex a husband needs in marriage is as common a problem today as it was two thousand years ago. And as is the case with most ageless problems, the issue is definitely complicated. But from the perspective of most men, it shouldn't be that way. What's complicated about a man and a woman enjoying sex with each other?

> At the time of marriage, most men consider frequent and fulfilling sex with their wives to be one of the God-given benefits of marriage. At that moment in time, most wives agree with their husbands. But as time passes, these men discover that their wives don't see things quite

the same way. They find that frequent sex requires nego-
tiation for which they apparently have no skill.[5]

The very thing that kills the sexual drive for a woman is when a
man stops making her feel cherished. He may do this gradually
or immediately. Some examples are:

- He doesn't affectionately touch her anymore during the day.
- He doesn't reach out to her in a crowd.
- He doesn't hold her elbow when they walk down the street.
- He doesn't put his arm around her when they are in a group or when they are in a line waiting for a movie to start.
- He doesn't kiss her on the neck or look adoringly at her and call her honey.
- He doesn't text her twenty times a day.
- He doesn't help her off with her coat.
- He doesn't open the door for her.
- He doesn't call her up every day.
- He doesn't ask her what she wants to do for fun.
- He doesn't plan a date for her.

Men do some or many of these wonderful things when courting but don't realize that these behaviors make a woman feel
cherished and are needed by the woman for a lifetime.

The hormone testosterone...which is in abundance in
most men...and in short supply in women, creates their
sexual craving. Women find that when they are admin-
istered the same amount of testosterone found in most

---

[5] Dr. Willard F. Harley Jr., "The Question of the Ages: How Can a Husband
Receive the Sex He Needs in Marriage?," Marriage Builders, accessed May 14,
2013, http://www.marriagebuilders.com/graphic/mbi8120_sex.html.

nineteen-year-old men, they too tend to have a craving for sex and find themselves searching for sexual relief as often as men.[6]

Silk On Fire is written for women who actually want to have that craving more often. If women could have that craving without tender attentiveness, dinner, flowers, phone calls, words of affection, and so on, they would take it! But without male testosterone, the female is left stumbling behind the male in desire. Women need to feel cherished to create the arousal that triggers the desire to have sex.

There has to be some clarity here. A man *thinking* that he is cherishing his wife and his wife actually *feeling cherished* can be two completely different things. I have heard husbands in marriage classes spout off to the group, "Oh, heck yeah, I cherish my lady!" With their arms around their women, they then spout off a couple of things they do while their wives smile sweetly. It just so happens that I personally have known those women, and they have told me that they didn't feel valued or respected at all by their husbands outside these marriage classes. I can almost guarantee these men have never asked their wives what would make them feel cherished and can guarantee they have forgotten how they "reeled in" their wives years before.

I know a man who was married for thirty years and bragged about never buying his wife flowers. I am sure she would have melted if he had ever gotten her even a single rose. He always said he knew what was best for her and believed that buying flowers was a waste of money (he had a fat bank account). He believed he always had a better idea of what loving her was than she did. That was not cherishing—that was selfish and controlling. Interestingly, they did not stay married.

One woman told me that she hated it when her husband started giving her foot rubs in bed. I said, "Are you crazy? Most women would want a foot rub."

---

[6] Ibid.

"But my husband only does it to get sex!" she responded.

"How do you know?" I asked her.

She said, "We have a mutual agreement not to have sexual intercourse during my period, and I have kept track. He never gives me a foot rub when I am *having* my period."

That certainly would send a clear message to a woman that the man is only offering the foot rubs to get what he knows he might get that night.

Do you know why women love the public show of attention by their husbands? Because they are in public and their husbands are showing affection, women rightly conclude that the attention has nothing to do with having sex at that moment. The husbands are doing it just to let their wives know they are attentive, not as a manipulation to have sex.

When a man responds in a way that makes his woman feel special, understood, listened to, and valued, he is showing her that she is cherished. I can hear readers saying, "Why are you not telling all this to our husbands?" I do tell men. But *this* book is written as a guide for women on how to crave sex with their husbands, and women have to take the following two steps:

First Step: Before women can convey to their husbands what they consider cherishing to be, they need to understand it themselves. This will take some introspective personal time.

Second Step: Women need to communicate this to their husbands. This will take time, patience, and persistence.

Two Exercises to Facilitate These Steps

Exercise #1. What did your husband do before your marriage that you really appreciated and that really attracted you to him? Make a list. It could be the way he opened the doors for you. It could be the way he introduced you. It could be the way he touched your arm as you went up or down stairs. It could be any of those things that made you feel valued. In other words, think about what he did to make you feel cherished enough to continue on in the relationship and eventually realize that you were in love.

Now add to that list of things other activities that he does now that you are married that make you feel cherished, very important in his life, and valued. Some examples are:

- You come home from work and he has vacuumed without being asked.
- He will do household chores and ask you, "What can I do for you today that will help you?"
- Every time you look at him at a party, he's looking at you.
- He tells the kids, "Mom is going to have some quiet time, so only come to me with your questions during the next two hours."
- He bathes your kids and puts them to bed, saying, "I'll run the bath for you, honey. You go relax."
- He says to you, "I'll look after the kids. You deserve a break!"
- He looks after the car maintenance.

Note any actions that he wouldn't be taking if he hadn't married you and was still single. Think about what it is that he does that makes you feel valued and makes you feel like he is attentive. When you think you are done, add at least ten more things to this list.

Shoes and Flowers

Of course both sexes need to feel cherished. I want to share a story that was told to me by Paddy Ducklow. He was counseling a couple who had come to him only because their son had begged them to. The situation had gotten so bad that the wife was living in the lower level of their home with their wheelchair-bound son and the husband was living upstairs. They had given up on ever reconciling but were staying together for the sake of their eighteen-year-old son. The son knew this and begged them to seek counseling, as he desperately wanted his folks *to want* to stay together. They reluctantly agreed.

Paddy said that when they entered his office, he saw a hardness and bitterness on each of their faces. He asked them if there was any reason that they wanted to stay together, and they both responded with a resounding "no!" They had only come for a one-time session to please their son.

Paddy then asked each of them this question: "If there was one tiny thing that you would want your spouse to do for you in the situation you are in at the moment, what would it be?"

It took both of them a while to actually come up with a suggestion. Annie said that she had never received flowers from Reg and that just receiving one flower daily would be nice. Reg agreed that he guessed he could do that.

After much thought, Reg mentioned that the entryway had a heater grate in it. He jogged early every morning and thought it would be quite nice to have his shoes on the grate every morning so that they would be warm when he slipped his feet into them to go jogging. Annie agreed to do this one small act each evening for him.

They agreed to return to Paddy's office in two weeks to analyze the outcome. As Annie came in the door two weeks later, she directed her angry stare at Paddy and said, "I hate you! I have begun to have feelings again. Now I have to deal with the fact that I care about Reg." And so began a series of counseling sessions that gave Annie and Reg the tools to repair, reconcile, and restore their marriage. It eventually evolved into a relationship that was far deeper and caring than ever before.[7] How amazing that

---

[7] Paddy Ducklow, in discussion with the author, February, 2008.

such a simple act, even though the idea was somewhat coerced and her husband did not initiate the idea to cherish her, could evoke such positive feelings in Annie.

Although both spouses need to know the other one is attentive, *being cherished is the motor* that drives a woman's sexual passion. It is the motor that drives a woman to sexually desire her husband.

Once you can articulate what makes you feel valued by your husband then, and only then, can you have a conversation with him and let him know what cherishing means to you and what it does for you.

Exercise #2. Let your husband know how important feeling cherished is. Let him know what attracted you to him. Once you know what it was that he did that made you feel valued, you can speak to him about it. This should not come across to him as something he needs to be doing because he's failing; instead, make it clear that this is something he has already done for you and is something you appreciate. First affirm for him what he has done, then explain that it is something that you still need in order to crave sex.

It is very important to have these conversations during the week because he wants sex during the week and you want to desire him sexually during the week. You're going to need to have this conversation often so that you can start to feel cherished during the week. Most men have difficulty "getting it." That is because they are wired differently.

Have this conversation regularly and in an affirming way, rather than in a critical, negative way. It is very important to begin this conversation when he's in the middle of doing something on one of these lists. You may have to wait for quite a while until he does it. You have to focus and be aware. If he rubs your feet, takes out the garbage, puts gas in the car, or does something else that's on your list, jump on it. Don't wait! Look at him, smile dreamily, be sincere (though you can also be dramatic), and tell him, "Honey, when you vacuum the living room without me nagging you, I feel valued. I feel more valued than if you bought me a piece of jewelry."

4

Then go up to him and give him a hug. Give him a kiss. Everyone needs to be rewarded at times. You won't get anywhere in your relationship if all you do is tell your husband what you want and remind him of what he is not doing without telling him what he is doing right. You might as well forget about having a successful conversation and growth in the relationship. Praising him will establish a pattern in his neurons that will help him to keep doing this. This will lead to you feeling more cherished later on.

How to Express Your Need to Be Cherished

If he goes on the defensive and gets hot and bothered, don't let your buttons get pushed. Relax, and then come back to the subject. Ask, "Do you want openness and honesty in our relationship?" (If he is not a jerk he will say yes.) "Can you understand that this is what I am trying to do? I am trying to be honest with you so that you can understand my needs. Am I right in thinking that you do want to fulfill my needs? I know I want to do the same with you."

If there has been a lot of anger between the two of you, with both of you playing the blame game, and if one of you always walks off in a huff, this exercise will have to be repeated several times. You will have to stand firm without getting exasperated before he actually trusts you not to fly off or withdraw from him.

Most couples just give up after their spouses disregard what they are saying or defend their actions. Often the only way a couple communicates is by shooting arrows and justifying their actions.

For successful communication, somebody has to stay calm, stay with the topic, be courageous, and take the defensive words for a few minutes without backing down. As Dr. Phil McGraw says, "Someone has to step up to the plate and be the hero. Why not you?"[8] Has your way been working for you? If not, then try a different way. If you try and he interrupts you, listen to him. If what he is saying has some measure of truth, admit it and tell him he has a valid point. Then ask him to listen and understand where you are coming from.

---

[8] Dr. Phil McGraw, *Dr. Phil*, Culver City, CA: Columbia Tristar Entertainment.

5

The Motor that Drives a Man to Cherish His Wife

IF THE MOTOR that drives a woman to have sex is feeling cherished, then what is the motor that drives a man to cherish a woman? *Sex is the motor* that drives most men to cherish their wives. The sexual experience that a man has with his wife is what drives him, encourages him, and motivates him to cherish his wife the way she wants to be cherished.

I imagine you're thinking, "Excuse me, Karen, but my man cherished me before we ever had sex." I am sure that is true. No woman would eagerly have sex with a man unless he has made her feel cherished. But the driving force behind him cherishing you was his desire to have a sexual relationship. This is how a man is created, and there is nothing wrong with it. He is designed to have this desire within him. He continued to court you and cherish you until he got you into his bed. After the sexual relationship has been embarked upon, he still wants to have sex, but the need to cherish you has diminished because he now has what he was after. I refer again to the quote from Harley's article:

> At the time of marriage, most men consider frequent and fulfilling sex with their wives to be one of the God-given benefits of marriage. At that moment in time, most wives agree with their husbands. But as time passes, these men discover that their wives don't see things quite the same way. They find that frequent sex requires negotiation for which they apparently have no skill."[9]

One day not so long ago, a young man was visiting me and showed interest in what I was writing about. I shared with him this concept of the motor that drives a man to cherish the woman he is with. He agreed that a man will impress his girlfriend and do everything to win her over so that he can enjoy a sexual relationship with her. In his case he only wanted the sexual relationship within marriage. Although he admitted that he wants and has always wanted more than just a sexual relationship in his marriage, sex is very important to him.

"I wanted to do everything I could to win her over, attract her, impress her," he said of his wife. "And why wouldn't I want my woman to feel as warm and loving *after* we are married as she did before? Why would I want to stop cherishing her? I am sexually fulfilled with her, and that motivates me to cherish her."

The conversation ended with me feeling encouraged that there are men out there who get it. I began telling him about an incident that happened in Edmonton, Alberta, when I was a teenager. In our neighborhood there was a family whose yard we could see from our backyard. We had a full view of their driveway and garage, which was thirty feet from our garage, if that. One of the family's sons was in his first year of college, and we often would see that young man cleaning and polishing his first car. He

---

[9] Harley, "The Question of the Ages."

would wash that car four times a week sometimes and buff it up with wax at least biweekly. He also had a girlfriend who would come over every Saturday. She'd lean up against the car and chat with him while he washed it. Sometimes we would even see her helping him buff it up.

One time my dad, mom, and I went out to our driveway to get into our vehicle and saw Steve washing his car again. My dad yelled to Steve, whose girlfriend was there helping him, "Well, Steve, I just hope that one day if you ever marry, you'll treat your wife as good as you treat that car." My dad just thought it was a truth that he was having fun with. And while my mom was embarrassed, it was a fantastic teaching moment for me. I don't know if Steve remembers that event, but I never forgot it.

When I told this story to this young husband, who had only been married for a few years, he said, "I get it! It's not like our wives are supposed to be treated like a possession or like a piece of machinery, but every day when I'm working in the bush, I look after my skidder. I always check it over to see if there are any cracks in the frame or any cracks on any part of the iron or steel that I need to look after. I'm always checking the tires. I'm always doing maintenance on it and making it sure it is well lubricated."

I asked him why he did that. He thought for just a moment before responding, "Well, because I don't want anything negative to happen to my valuable machinery and I certainly don't want anything to seize up. It makes the whole illustration of cherishing my wife come to light. My wife is not a piece of machinery, nor do I see her as a possession, but if I value her, why wouldn't I want to treat my wife as well as I treat a piece of machinery for my business?"

"Well yes, you don't want your wife to seize up one day," I said.

"No, I don't want to come home and find her breaking down or gone. I want to come home and have satisfying sex with her. That satisfying sex motivates me to listen to her and try to meet her emotional needs."

I thought, "Wow, he does get it!"

The unfortunate thing is that some of you are in a relationship right now where you don't feel valued. In fact, some of you are even being abused. You may have married a man who charmed you into marriage or the relationship that you're in and then completely stopped making you feel valued. You may even think that something is wrong with you because you didn't see this coming. You were deceived and made a bad choice, but I want you to know that that doesn't make you a less valuable person. You are staying with him because you believe that he is going to change. He won't.

When you are with an abuser and he's hurting you physically, emotionally, and verbally, you need to get professional counseling that will help you get away from the danger. He's not going to change. You need to get out of that relationship.

If you're not living with an abuser but are simply living with someone who has forgotten how to make women feel valued, remember that that can change with informative communication. If your spouse is still alive, it's not too late.

Although I have discussed some ways of communicating, I highly recommend reading *Essential Elements of Sex* by Erin Faye and *His Needs/Her Needs* by Dr. Willard F. Harley Jr. I also recommend Dr. Harley's workbook, *5 Steps To Romantic Love*.

6

A Man Asks His Woman for Sex; How Does She Ask to Be Cherished?

ALTHOUGH GENEVIEVE, A young woman of twenty-eight, would say that she is happily married to her husband, Hans, thirty-two, she knows there has been something simmering in their lives in the last three weeks. Genevieve has not been interested in sex for some time. They have three children. Genevieve is a stay-at-home mom, and her husband is a successful businessman with a lot on his mind. Hans has a thriving business that needs a lot of his time.

Hans is home every night, and his sex drive has never waned. He's trying to be respectful because he knows that Genevieve is not really responding to his sexual advances when he reaches out to her at night for the sexual relationship that he wants. She turns over every time he reaches for her, and he doesn't want to push her. He wants to be a good lover but also has a need for sex.

Genevieve knows that they should have sex for the good of their marriage but is actually angry every time he reaches for her and doesn't know why. All she knows is her sex drive is low and she's not feeling the way she wants to toward her husband's advances.

Finally, after Genevieve rejects Hans for the umpteenth time, he says to her, "Honey, I know you don't seem to want to have sex, and I'm sorry. I want to be a better husband but I just need it. I have this strong sexual desire and am starting to lust after other women in the office. I don't want them, I want you, but this happens when I haven't had sex with you for a long time."

In the back of her mind, Genevieve knows that things like that do happen. She even had a neighbor who had that happen in her marriage. Her friend stopped having sex with her husband, and eight months later he was in a full-fledged sexual affair. That is not what she wants, and although she is not intrigued with the idea of sex, she concedes because she wants the best for her marriage.

They have intercourse, and he has an orgasm. He's relieved but feels bad because he knows she hasn't gotten anything out of it. He doesn't know what to do about it, so he turns over and goes to sleep. She is troubled, annoyed, and almost sick to her stomach. She feels like she has to give sex to her husband because he has started to lust after other women.

Now let's turn the tables. How does she tell him that she needs to be cherished because she is lusting after other men? It's the afternoon, and she stands in front of him and says, "Hon, I have not been feeling cherished for the past few weeks and I'm starting to lust after other men. I really need to feel cherished right now." It just doesn't sound the same.

When a man states he is not having enough sex, his woman immediately knows what he is referring to. "I'm lusting after women in the office." That's clear! "I am vulnerable to an affair." That's even clearer! But if a woman states, "I haven't felt cherished for the last three weeks," the man will be confused.

And if she says, "It's making me lust after other men. "I really need it now," he will think one of three things:

1. She wants to have sex with me tonight!
2. All right. We can have sex tonight!

3. I am going to get lucky tonight!

How does a man immediately make his wife feel cherished so that she will stop lusting after other men? Although good men will agree that women should be treated equally and fairly and that both men and women have an equal need, they may not realized that women's needs are so much more involved. To men, the sex can be asked for and given in one twenty-minute event or less, and it is an act that satisfies men's needs immediately. Most women don't even know what it is they are feeling. They don't know they are vulnerable to other men, and this brings me to the rest of Genevieve's story.

Three days after Genevieve and her husband had intercourse, their carpenter comes to work on their house. He is a single friend around Genevieve's age, and as he works, they talk. Later she serves him lunch. During this time he comments on her amazing organizational skills, which he notices while in the home. He praises her for the amazing meal that she has just served him.

In helping him move things, she slips, and he catches her by the elbow. He is sincerely concerned about whether she is all right. He makes sure she sits down and checks to make sure she hasn't sprained her ankle. He takes a look at it. At this point there is nothing inappropriate happening, but she's vulnerable. She hasn't felt cherished by her husband for some time. This carpenter has been valuing her mind and her skills over the past few days, and now he is showing her concern. He's being attentive. He's listening to her. He's touching her. He's cherishing her! He is new, and that is an exciting thing in itself. It's an affair waiting to happen. What needs to change so this won't end badly?

Open dialogue is needed. A woman cannot have a productive conversation with her husband about not feeling cherished if she has never before explained what she needs to her husband. And she certainly cannot articulate what she needs if she has never articulated it to herself.

Many times a woman will feel angry when her husband reaches out and coerces her into having sex. I don't mean an act of rape; I'm referring to when a woman feels a strong sense of obligation to perform a service for her husband so he doesn't feel lust for other women. Is that really her responsibility?

It is the responsibility of both spouses to fulfill the needs of the other so they don't feel the need for or fall vulnerable to other people. It is so much more difficult and complicated for the woman to convey her needs, but it has to be done or she will not get what she wants, which is to actually crave sex with her husband.

A woman speaks more words during a day than a man, which is a fact people laugh about it. The subject is the brunt of jokes. It's OK to laugh about it, but you should also start using your God-given ability to communicate and use it to your advantage. For example, have a weekly conversation with your husband about feeling cherished. Just explain what it means to you to be cherished. Your husband will become more familiar with the term and begin to understand what you are talking about. This is so much more productive than blowing up at him once a year or monthly about something that gets way out of hand (he thinks) and making him feel attacked. That certainly doesn't help you.

If you haven't been craving sex and your libido is low, you obviously have not been feeling cherished. It's time to change this. During one of the serious conversations that you should be having two or three times a week, simply say, "I'm feeling vulnerable in our relationship, honey. I'm not ready to go out and look for a man—that's not what I'm saying. But the other day, when I was at the office, one of our lawyers just listened to me in a really sweet way. He seemed interested in me and asked me questions about the company. It made me feel really smart. Then he asked me to have lunch with him to finish the conversation. He even held my coat for me. You know, it made me sort of feel giddy, and at that moment I realized that I'm vulnerable to an attraction. Can we talk about that? Can we talk about what will make me feel cherished so that I'm not open to other men cherishing me?" What real husband could say no to that conversation if it is delivered without anger or blame?

Please note that there's nothing wrong with a man helping another man's wife with her coat or giving her a compliment about how nice she looks in a dress at a party. There's nothing wrong with that, but if the woman's husband has not complimented her in months or years, she's very vulnerable to getting "reeled in" when any man tells her how good she looks. The vulnerability is the fault of the couple, not the gentleman who is being sincere.

Through the ages our culture has accepted the idea that a woman either gets a man who understands her, cherishes her, and is sweet to her or she doesn't. Women who don't get such a man must live with who they have and just suck it up. And a man either gets a woman who is hot for him sexually and stays hot for him or he doesn't. If it's the latter, he has to live with it. But this doesn't have to be.

Marriage involves continuing education. The two people must continue to educate each other on the proper way to treat each other. Why does anyone settle? It's ridiculous! The key to hot fulfilling sex for both partners is for the woman to understand what being cherished is and for her husband to believe and understand that he needs to give this to his wife in order for him to have more sex and a more fulfilling sexual relationship.

It is not just giving something, it is doing something. It's responding, and it's the man valuing his wife. When a husband and wife have sexual intercourse, the husband feels valued. His self-esteem goes up. I have had young and senior men say to me that sex makes them feel secure in their relationship.

For a woman, sexual intercourse doesn't make her feel valued or secure unless she is feeling cherished already. Then the lovemaking is a conclusion to her cherishing. But to a man, it can be an introduction and a conclusion; it's like the act says it all for a man—or for most men, at least.

I have heard other men say that their biggest need isn't sexual, it's receiving affirmation. Receiving affirmation is huge in their life. In my conversations with these men, we eventually come full circle as they realize that the sexual act with their wives is the most important affirmation of all. Therefore, I have to conclude that the sexual act is an affirmation to the man. It verifies that he's valued and strong and raises his self-esteem. But the sex act by itself for a woman is not that at all. She needs to feel valued and cherished in order to crave and desire sex.

The Allen Wrench Method

At this point I am reminded that there are men out there who just will not "get it." Their wives have sought the help of coaches and counselors and tried out ideas they read about or heard about on TV to motivate their husbands to cherish them and thus reignite their fire. Nothing has worked. It is at this point that I would suggest using the Allen Wrench Method (AWM).

An Allen Wrench is a wrench that looks like an L. The wrench is used to get at small screws that cannot be grabbed by other wrenches. A person holds the wrench by the long end and places the short end into the difficult-to-reach small space to release the screw. Sometimes a wife may need to apply the AWM to receive what she emotionally and physically needs.

Years ago the church where my husband is a pastor invited Allan Dunbar, another pastor of a church in Calgary, to speak in our community. I had asked him if he would speak to the women at a women's luncheon that we were having that weekend. He said he would be glad to.

I really don't remember the topic that I gave him or what we agreed that he would speak on, but I believe it was rather broad. I was quite surprised when he honed in on and began to speak about wife-husband relations. I remember him saying the following: "A woman doesn't realize the power she has after a good lovemaking session with her husband. At this time she can basically ask anything and will ultimately receive some kind of positive response, usually resulting in receiving what she asked for."

He then went on to encourage us women "to use this prime time for requesting what we needed as women in the husband and wife relationship and for requesting both emotional and material things."[10]

I must say my mouth dropped. I had heard women allude to this, but to actually have a man teach this to us was new and shocking in a refreshing way. Since then I have experimented with this, and it has always proved true.

I call it the Allen Wrench Method because of Allan Dunbar and the Allen wrench example.

The Allen Wrench Method is great for all couples, even if the wife is already feeling cherished and craving sex without it. It is a wonderful, honest way to receive even more. If a husband has the resources to give his wife what she asks for, he will! And the odd thing is that even though the husband is well aware that a wife is taking advantage of an opportune moment, the husband doesn't feel manipulated. Therefore, women are crazy not to use such a powerful moment to their advantage.

The important thing I would add to all this is that this is not a good time to criticize, analyze, or launch into a huge lecture. Lecturing is an absolute no-no! Just cheerfully be succinct and brief. If your husband likes to talk after sex (there are some who do), then that can be a time when you can share with your husband what being cherished means to you and how you need it in order to crave sex with him. But don't let it become a long, drawn-out analysis. Be brief, and always end on what he is doing right that attracts

---

[10] Allan Dunbar, in discussion with the author, (1980?).

you and arouses you. Remember, "While criticism causes men to become defensive, *admiration energizes and motivates them.*"[11]

Should you only have sex so you can ask for something personal? Absolutely not! I am writing to women who want to desire and appreciate sex more with their mates. Use the moment to express your requests when and if you want anything, and it will result in you being cherished.

I can hear readers asking, "So what you're saying is that I have to give him sex in order for him to make me feel cherished?" The answer is no. A woman won't automatically feel cherished because she agrees to sex, but neither will she be cherished by her husband if she withholds the sex. Remember what drives a man to cherish the woman he is with. Here is the formula:

> **A woman will be more successful in asking for what she wants if she does so after a good lovemaking session than any other time.**

Tell him what you enjoyed about making love with him. Let him know that you want more of the same thing. Without using the word "but," share with him what the motor is (feeling cherished) that drives you to want sex. It is very important here to communicate with him without attaching blame. The best time to communicate all this is after sex, while you're tracing you fingers over his back. If he falls asleep right away after sexual intercourse, the next day tell him you want to book some special time with him. Plan to get away privately at lunch time or after work, when he's not in a hurry. You see, you are building on the successful time that you both had together to inform him about how you can crave sex with him more.

---

[11] Dr. Willard F. Harley Jr., *His Needs, Her Needs* (Tarrytown: Fleming H. Revell Company, 1986).

6

This is not manipulation. It is choosing the best and smartest time to communicate with him. It would be manipulation if you decided to have sex *in order* to get what you want; instead you are *using the most powerful time* to communicate what you need now. Think of it not as giving so you can get, but as using the time that you've had together sexually to enlighten your partner so you both can have your needs met more fully.

But be prepared, as most women will have to use this powerful time to communicate the same thing more than once before they get what they are asking for. Therefore, the more times you have sex in a week, the greater chance you will have of effectively communicating what you need.

When a man hears, "Honey, I believe in you," and his woman's actions prove it, he will go to the ends of the Earth for her. If she affirms his ideas and builds him up by listening and asking questions about his goals and dreams, she is "proving it." When a man feels respected, he will be more willing to take suggestions.

I highly recommend the book *Love and Respect* by Dr. Emerson Eggerichs.[12] It speaks to the distinct responses that spouses can give to each other to improve their communication.

Women, you need to "get it." Your husband will never learn from you unless you get it. Your husband can even read this book, but unless you get it and start communicating with him and sharing with him what it means to you to feel valued, you can't blame him. You can never blame him again for making you feel obligated about sex, for not loving you the way you need, for not hearing you, and for not being the gentleman or the tenderhearted, charming man you fell in love with or thought you were getting.

Realize that feeling cherished is the motor that will drive your sexual passion. Communicate this to your husband so you can then move ahead with being totally loved the way you want to be loved by your man and begin craving the sex you both want.

---

[12] Dr. Emerson Eggerichs, *Love & Respect: The Love She Most Desires, The Respect He Desperately Needs* (Brentwood: Integrity Publishers, 2004).

7

A Woman's Largest Sex Organ

A WOMAN'S LARGEST SEX organ is her brain. The brain has more to do with sexual success in a woman than it does in a man. If a woman hasn't had success in achieving orgasm, she may not be looking forward to sexual activity with her husband and often feels hopeless. Some women haven't been able to have enough success and climax only occasionally. These women are also discouraged and don't look forward to lovemaking.

The brain's neurons have to experience success in order for the neurotransmitters to latch onto the neurons. Neurons are nerve cells that gather and transmit electrochemical signals to different parts of your body. So you have to train the neurons of your brain to have success, and that success will release chemicals in the brain to trigger arousal.

"For many years researchers believed that the brain stopped changing. At a certain age, the theory went, we possessed all of the neurons and the neural connections that we'd ever have.

Now, neuroscientists know that the brain can continue to change even as we age, a concept known as neuroplasticity."[13]

The brain likes change but will only change once a thought process has started. The brain has to believe, and all belief has to do with the thought process. A person has to start the belief process with a thought. Intellectually, a woman has to want to desire her husband and have faith that she will be able to climax. This then is transmitted to the neurons, which begin to change their pathway in order to execute the thought. So a woman intellectually has to trust that there is hope and that something is going to happen in her love life in order for it to actually happen. She has to put those thoughts into play in her brain.

Until the neurons in the brain actually register the fact that she has had an orgasm, they are going to be resistant to allowing her to have success. It seems odd, but it's true. Therefore, a woman has to go into the belief area of the brain and force the neurons along different pathways in order to achieve success. Then it will be easier the next time. A woman needs to take time to focus her thoughts. The woman's brain will pick this up, and she will actually begin to believe that there is going to be something better.

Many women approach the sex act with a mind-set of "this is never going to get better." In order to change she has to focus and make herself believe that it's going to get better. In my Silk On Fire™ workshops, I really take time to discuss how to develop good tools that help women intentionally focus so they can achieve success.

A woman also has to know, "I am attractive, I am sexy, and I am desirable." Often a woman's brain battles one or more of these three areas every day. Most women struggle with body image issues. As part of my passion coaching, I share methods with women for training the brain to hope for a better sex life and to believe that they are attractive, desirable, and sexy.

---

[13] *Curiosity.com*, "What is Neuroplasticity?," http://curiosity.discovery.com/question/what-is-neuroplasticity (accessed August 8, 2012).

In the next chapter, you will learn how to train your brain to improve your body image and how to believe in yourself. Most women I talk to don't have a good body image. I know there are women who do feel good, but most are critical about their bodies.

You have to start looking at your body the way your husband positively looks at your body. He thinks you are fantastic naked. He thinks you are beautiful and desirable naked. So if he thinks that, why can't you think that? He is the one you want to impress, right? Women keep comparing their own bodies to somebody else's in some movie, show, or magazine. Doing so rips them apart. Women need to stop the madness. Yes, they should definitely want to keep up their health with wise food choices, exercise, and sleep. But they should be grateful for what they have and be absolutely excited about the fact that their husbands see them as so desirable. That's the bottom line, isn't it?

I think every woman reading this book wants to have hot, fulfilling sex with her husband. A woman may have faltered and had an affair with somebody else, but I don't think that's what she set out to do. I think women get married because they want the sanctity of marriage. They want the intimacy, trust, and privacy that this wonderful union gives them with their husbands. This is why women should celebrate it and quit putting their husbands down for loving their naked bodies.

Right here I want to clarify that I know there are husbands who actually criticize their wives' looks and say things like, "Your weight is a problem," "Your butt is too flat," and "Wear makeup when you go out with me." These statements would challenge any woman's self-esteem. If you are in this tough situation, you have three choices:

1. You can change if you want to (and if it is something you can actually change) and then tell them to be quiet about it.
2. You can explain to him that those remarks hurt you and that you would appreciate it if they were removed from his vocabulary.

3. If it continues, you will have to realize that you have a verbally abusive husband, which this book cannot speak to. Get good, professional counsel immediately.

More about Brain Power

Women have said to me, "But if I light the candles in the bedroom, he'll think automatically that we're going to have sex, and I don't want him to automatically think that." Then I ask the question, "Is it that you don't want to have sex, or is it that you don't want to give him sex *just because that's what he wants?* I detect in the above statement that your brain is in a power struggle between what your husband wants and what you want in the relationship. If you want to crave sex, wouldn't you want to be pleasured?"

This is not a power struggle. I repeat, sexual pleasuring is not a power struggle. Put aside your differences during lovemaking. You have to change your perception. Sex is about you, *the beautiful wife*, being pleasured. Don't approach it like you are "giving only to him," "servicing him," and "giving him what he has been wanting." Why wouldn't *you* want to be sexually pleasured *by him*? You should want to "come in through the front door." You need to change your perception of the act. For instance, if before he could even wonder why you are lounging there so seductively in your sexy lingerie you said to him, "What do you have for me tonight baby?" (instead of "Don't even think about it!"), wouldn't that change your perception? This is called "coming in through the front door" for women and should be done instead of begrudgingly responding when men hint that they want sex.

When an insensitive man notices his wife in her lingerie, it is possible that he will begin to immediately mount the lady, but then the lady needs to say, "No, love." If this happens to you, always respond with a grin. You can say, "Honey, I want to be pleasured by my lover first; that would be you pleasuring me. Then I'll give you yours, and this is how I like it." Then talk sexy and show him. "Neuroscientific research indicates that experience can actually change both the brain's physical structure and functional organization."[14] You have to work to get the neurotransmitters to release the chemicals you need in order to trigger arousal. If this becomes a habit, the neurons will get rerouted and you will become aroused more easily.

Eventually, this will become a really good automatic habit. You won't think of it anymore as serving or making him happy. You will think of it as, "I am going to be pleasured tonight!" It's all about you; you've got to get your brain reconditioned in order to crave sex.

[14] *Wikipedia*, "Neuroplasticity," http://en.wikipedia.org/wiki/Neuroplasticity (accessed August 8, 2012).

8

Building the Fire

ANY WOMAN WHO has been successful with having an orgasm will also know that she will not automatically sustain a high sexual libido in the different seasons of her life. There have to be other factors involved in her life. So far two factors that are required in order for a woman to crave sex with her husband have been mentioned:

1. Being able to achieve orgasm
2. Being cherished by her husband

There are two other factors that, when combined with the above factors, will up a woman's sexual drive on an ongoing basis and keep her craving sex with her spouse.

Even if you know how to have orgasm and your husband knows how to give you an orgasm and is very affectionate, you will find that there will be periods when you have a lower sex drive. It might help you to develop two more areas of your life:

3. Focusing on yourself as a feminine, sexual being.
4. Scheduling alone time with your husband (not just for lovemaking).

Developing these two areas will keep you *attracted* to your husband. (The key word here is "attracted," not "attractive." There is a big difference.)

Focusing and Scheduling Will Help Up Your Sexual Libido

Women really need to cultivate a good sex life with their husbands. In North America, how to cultivate a good sex life in marriage is not a common subject, and women who focus on themselves as sexual beings are often only found in tasteless and often bizarre media.

Why is it so very important that women spend time thinking about themselves as sexual beings? Since it is so intimate, women are the only ones who can hold themselves accountable for its fitness. Sex is a part of who they are and is supposed to be acted on in the marital relationship.

Why don't women focus on sexual fitness? The biggest obstacle is that it takes a lot of personal reflection and is most often viewed by others as being a self-centered activity. Some women were conditioned to believe that concentrating on sex is wrong or at best frivolous.

Even women who don't feel guilty or self-centered may consider such focus to be unproductive. They may think that sex is something you automatically are "fit" at or not. Sex has never been considered something women should be intentional about or discipline themselves to get better at.

Asking a woman to take time out of her week to look after herself in any way with no one else involved is a very new concept. Actually scheduling personal time on a calendar is not something that has been spoken about until lately. Holidays and taking breaks have been around, but not "me time."

I want to go deeper into the core of the female who wants to up her libido. Not only does a woman need to take time out for herself to rest and to relax, but she also needs to take time out so that she can be sexual. A woman needs to take time to actually think about herself as a hot, sexy woman. How does she do this? It wasn't very difficult when she was younger, if her hormones were raging, and there was a young man she liked who was attracted to her. It wasn't difficult to feel sexual then, but it also was new.

As spoken about earlier in this book, newness ties into infatuation. It's actually not love, but instead is the newness that attracts women. They can't get the newness back into their relationship. They can never again feel the anticipation they felt before they first had sex with their husbands. But they all want to feel that sexy desire again, so how do they do that? They have to learn to concentrate on their sexuality in order for it to rise to the surface again. Focusing on their sexuality will help bring about the hot, sexy feelings for their husbands.

Scheduling Time to Focus on Sexuality

Training your brain to improve your body image will ultimately improve your sexual body image. Women actually have to schedule time for meditating on their sexuality; it won't just happen. One of the biggest impediments to setting aside time to focus in on sexuality is that there are so many other things in women's lives to schedule in.

If you find this to be the case, remember that in order to make time to focus in on yourself, you have to make the *decision* to plan. *Plan* to have an afternoon when you are just going to think of yourself as a sexual being. *Schedule* it on your calendar. Then *focus* on yourself.

You might have a long hot bath. You might get a sexy novel out. You might just do a pedicure and manicure and think about the last time you had amazing sex with your husband.

Let's say you schedule it for a Thursday afternoon, well in advance. You have also planned for your sister to pick up the kids. One week before 'your afternoon' your friends decide to plan a birthday party for another mutual friend on that same afternoon. Now, everyone will understand if you can't attend because of having to take your child to his hockey practice, but who will understand if you tell them that you are actually going to take some time out to think about yourself as a hot, sexy woman?

Of course, you won't be telling anyone what you are actually doing, but you live in a world that makes you feel like you have to justify why you are not attending a friend's birthday party. You are the only one who can be strong and keep this commitment to yourself. You're the only one who can say, "I have an important appointment that has been booked for weeks. I'm sorry, I can't make the party."

A man thinks about sex with his wife for days after he has had a hot evening with her. Most women will cringe as they think, "Oh, we actually did that?" They may even be embarrassed thinking about it, but men actually spend time thinking about themselves as lovers and about how everything was so fantastic. Most women just move on. However, there is a place in their brains for meditating about being sexual, and this is what they need to cultivate.

Let me tell you Suzan's story. Suzan had been away on a trip from her husband for ten days and was returning home. She realized that she was eagerly anticipating returning home to her lover's arms. She fantasized while sitting on the plane about how their first night was going to be.

She became so aroused thinking about it that she devised a plan to surprise her husband with a real hot striptease sometime. She wanted to do it for her husband with all the props and music. She told me that it was so thrilling to think about and that she even chose the music for it. She said that after she got home, it took her a couple of weeks to get everything together. She even bought a pole that fit in her bedroom for the pole dance. She bought long sexy black gloves that reached her elbows and black stockings that were held up with a camisole and garters. She even bought some sexy black high heels just for the occasion. She had a list and did her shopping. As the day got closer, she had reached a new height of sexual excitement.

Suzan and Jack had four children. She farmed the kids out that evening, and he didn't know what hit him when the music went on and the dance began. Eight years later, her husband still refers to that pole dance that she did. He gets excited every time he thinks of it. The point here is that she told me she did it for herself. When she was planning the event, she got aroused every time she thought about it and purchased something to carry out her plan. Although she did it for herself, it was a gift to her husband too.

This is the beauty of such a plan. Every time a woman carries out a sexual fantasy for herself within the marriage, her husband is fulfilled as well. As women know all too well, it doesn't work too well the other way! If a husband surprised his wife with, "Tonight, dear, I want you to put on these clothes and do a pole dance for me," she would want to slap his face.

First make the *decision* to *plan* and *schedule* your alone time. Then *focus* in on yourself and your sexuality. This will lead to another *decision* to *schedule couple time.*

Diagram 3: Cycle of Intention

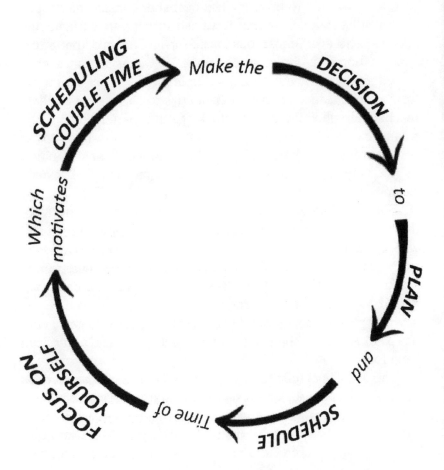

Illustrated by Andrew Willis

SCHEDULE 1

cusing on yourself" happen? I already discussed
e alone. You need to put it on your calendar. In
'M workshops I actually provide a yearly calen-
times get their own day planners out and spend
uling in an afternoon or morning for themselves
ould be two hours or an entire afternoon. During
nt to think of yourself as very, very sexy.

FOCUS EXERCISE 1

You want to stop looking at your flaws and start looking at yourself the way your husband looks at you. I suggest that you take a warm bubble bath using all your favorite products—scented soap, bath lotion, facial masks, body scrubs, etc. Have soft music playing in the background. You need to be alone; you cannot have your children outside knocking on the door.

Women ask me, "Karen, do you actually do this?" Yes, I actually do this. That's why I know it works! I tell my family, "I need a particular afternoon off, so you all better plan somewhere else to go. You better plan another office to be at and take your book somewhere else because you won't be allowed in between one o'clock and five o'clock." I lock the door. I turn the phone off. I guard that time, as it is so important! They don't know what I am doing (at least they didn't until I wrote this book!); they just know that I am enjoying "me time."

You may decide to spend the afternoon looking for sexy lingerie. Maybe you don't even have the money for it, but you can go out, window shop, and fantasize about buying some expensive lingerie. Maybe all you will buy is a new lipstick or some mood music, but you'll take some time to absolutely think of yourself in a sexual way. Decide to dress up that day with heels and a skirt. You don't necessarily have to dress in a fancy way, but rather in a very womanly, sexy way. Are you trying to draw attention to yourself? No, but there's nothing like a few male eyes looking your way to give you a boost. It's more about getting yourself in a zone. You might decide that this is the day that you will take off to go and get your hair trimmed and then meet your husband at your favorite restaurant.

If you are a busy mom who can only manage to get someone to watch your children for two hours or a woman who is really stretching those pennies and is on a tight budget, that's OK. You don't have to spend a lot of money. Use your home. Create a mini-spa in your own tub. Use anything you've got in your closet.

Look at yourself in the mirror. Begin to see yourself the way your husband does. Look at yourself through his sensuous eyes. So many times women don't even want to look at themselves naked in a mirror or in sexy lingerie. Well, if you are one of those women, it's time to turn over a new leaf. Do you want to improve your sex life? Then you have got to change. You can't keep doing the same thing you've been doing, as it's not working; otherwise, why would you be reading this book?

Write a sexy story with you and your husband as the main characters. Use your sex toys. You might have bought something at one time that you never really learned how to use or are too embarrassed to use with your husband. This is the time. Try out another lubricant. Some women masturbate to the second level of arousal to get themselves excited for their husbands when they come home.

Take out some sexy novels from the library. Get as many informational books as you can on sex. I am not referring to or suggesting pornography. Even though there may be topics in books that you don't agree with or are uncomfortable with, just close them up and allow yourself to fantasize. It is very important for you to read about sexuality. This is a good time to read about your physical body having an orgasm and to concentrate on sexuality by reading about. Having conversations with other wives that you trust will create a greater connection to your sexuality and raise your sexual libido. This will cause you to be able to connect better with your husband. In other words, reading about sexuality, reading about sexual fulfillment, and talking to other women about what works for them can be very positive for you and your sexual relationship with your husband. It will propel you forward in passion and desire.

When was the last time you sat around with a group of women and listened to some healthy sex talk? After I present at one of my Silk On Fire™ workshops, women are always giggling afterward and saying that they can't wait to go home to their husbands because just listening to the information got them so sexually excited. What that tells me is that women need to do that more. They need to talk together and urge each other on in the sexual arena.

Visit my website to see my free bonus, "Answers to Ten Questions Most Women Ask." www.silkonfirebook.com

FOCUS EXERCISE 2

Now that you have focused on yourself as sexual, beautiful, and attractive, spend some time thinking about what attracts or attracted you to your husband. Even though you both may have changed physically through the years, there is probably something that you still find attractive and that would attract you if you just met your husband under different circumstances. Be assured (or beware) that there are women out there who are presently attracted to your husband. Think of your husband as a man who is wanted by other women. Take out a piece of paper, and write down all the fabulous things about your husband. Include anything you find attractive (believe me, other women will have thought of it). Here's a suggestion list to get you going:

long, dark eyelashes	thick, wavy hair
impressive body strength	bald head
muscular biceps	built like a bull
muscular thighs	lean and tall
toned butt	short and wiry
nice skin tone	humorous
the way he speaks	has a great voice
perfect white teeth	plays an instrument

charming, crooked smile	totally respects me
the way he laughs	a true gentleman
strong hands	witty
people smart	intelligent in business
makes good money	knows what I like

Write all those things down that could be characteristics that a woman finds sexy. Let your imagination go (and let go of the last time you argued). If the last time you thought of him was in angry terms, do a mind cleanse. Perhaps you both haven't made a move to have sex with each other for a long time, so you have to get your mind out of the groove it's in and put it in a new groove. (See the free bonus article on my website called, "Not This Year Darling".)

This isn't silly; it's about directing the way you want your mind to work. Do you want it to work in a boring, critical way or make it go along a groove so that you can have a hot, sexy date every night (or at least once a week)?

It's a fact that the newness cannot be recaptured but you can, enter into a deeper level of intimacy, and have a lot of fun doing different things. Instead of trying to look for that newness and being disappointed because it's not there, build on your successes. Think about the last times when sex was good. Think about what you did, what he did, and how he did it to get yourself hot and sexy during this time of focusing on yourself. You cannot have the infatuation again, but you can stimulate those sexual feelings.

SCHEDULE 2

This begins with securing time for lovemaking. It's simple, but you have to schedule it in on your calendars. Take an hour to sit down and take turns rubbing each other's feet (or giving one another a massage wherever the other one likes it). As you give each other those wonderful massages, plan your schedule for the month. It's your lovemaking plan. I really think it's interesting when women come up to me after I speak on this and ask, "What about the spontaneity?"

"What about it?" I usually respond. "Are you having it? Are you having lots of wonderful, spontaneous, hot times?" And they laugh, look away, and shuffle their feet. Of course spontaneity is great! There is nothing wrong with spontaneity, but don't count on it. When you and your husband were dating or first becoming attracted to each other, were your get-togethers spontaneous? They certainly weren't! There had to be a communication. Somebody had to phone somebody and plan a get together. Whether you went out to the movies, a hockey game, or supper, there had to be a plan, and as part of that plan, both of you were seeking each other's attention.

After you both have agreed upon the scheduling, you need to be tough. You may have to be the administrator and make sure your husband holds to the plan. That's just the way it is with most couples, but don't let it get under your skin. As long as you both agree on your personal schedules and work to protect your schedules, it doesn't really matter who administrates the family's schedule around this, as long as it is adhered to.

Here I want to clarify the difference between planning and scheduling. Scheduling is planning, but planning is not necessarily scheduling. Let me share an example. On Sunday, Melissa decided she would focus in on herself on her day off next week. She thought she would try to take a few hours in the morning. Although it was ten days away, the thought of relaxing in a hot bubble bath while thinking sexy thoughts brought a smile to her face.

At work on Monday, her boss asked her if she would be willing to help out with the latest volunteer work their team was doing at the soup kitchen at noon the following week. She loved the company's policy of volunteering more in the community and said she would love to be at the soup kitchen at two o'clock on Wednesday to prepare for the next day's meal. Later that evening she realized that that was the day she was going to take off to focus on herself. "Oh well, I probably could do both," she thinks.

A few days later, her son called to ask if she could look after his two toddlers for a couple of hours while he went to the dentist. He had made an appointment the week before (but had forgotten to mention it to her earlier) and would have to bring them over at around eleven o'clock on Wednesday morning. She felt she couldn't say no, and there went her plan down the drain!

That was planning. Now here is the same example again, only with scheduling instead of planning. On Sunday, Melissa decided to focus in on herself on her day off the following week. She got her day planner out, confirmed that she had nothing else planned, and wrote in "focus" for Wednesday, the twentieth. She highlighted the date on her kitchen calendar and on her cell phone. Although it was ten days away, the thought of relaxing in a hot bubble bath while thinking sexy thoughts brought a smile to her face. She decided to phone Ken, her son, and let him know that just in case he might be counting on her for Wednesday to look after the grandchildren for anything, she wouldn't be available.

At work on Monday, her boss asked her if she would be willing to help out with the latest volunteer work their team was doing at the soup kitchen at noon the following week. She loved their company's policy of volunteering more in the community and said, "I would love to, but let me check my schedule first." She realized that that was her day to focus on herself, and although she had booked her focus time for the morning, she decided to play it safe and secure the whole day, planning nothing else. "Sorry," she told him, "I am booked for that day." Later in the week, when her son realized he needed a babysitter, he remembered that his mom had told him she was booked on Wednesday. He would have to find someone else besides his mom. Melissa never got a call from him, so she never had to feel obliged to say yes. Melissa had secured her plan by scheduling, and the only things that went down her drain were bubbles and water!

Once you've planned it, schedule it in so that it becomes a solid event you can see when checking the calendar for other dates instead of just an idea in your mind that gets pushed around when other people pull at you. Hold on to that plan. Secure it when people call. When you make appointments with dentists and doctors, do it around your focus time. Keep scheduling this time in every month until it becomes a way of life. Don't put it on the back burner.

You also need to communicate all of this to your husband. Speak to him about it in a very soft way. Ask him to help secure and protect this time for you. It could go something like this: "Honey, I want to please you and I want to be hot for you. [After being successful at climaxing, you will be confident that you will be hot for him.] But I need some time alone, away from everyone. I need you to look after the children for a couple of hours or help me find someone who will." It is a rare man who would not move heaven and Earth to help his wife secure time for the sole purpose of getting in touch with her sexuality in order to be sensuous and passionate about their love life. A man will make a sacrifice if he knows it is going to work.

When your husband experiences the change in you, he will be motivated and will continue doing whatever it takes to help you secure this time. During this time it's very important to think of your husband when you are fantasizing. But beware! If you use this time to watch your favorite show on TV, talk on the phone to your friend, bake, or clean, you are not going to be fulfilling what you set out to do, and that would be deceptive. Your husband will find that it's not making any difference. If you do it the right way, it will up your sex drive.

These are the extra factors and steps you must take to up your sexual libido: you need to focus on yourself as a sexual woman and communicate with your husband about how to schedule and secure time for lovemaking.

9

Fifteen Hours

ONE OF THE best activities Ian and I ever did together was playing tennis one summer. I think we played it together only once. I had played it in high school and loved it. He had never played it. Ian had not played many things because he had joyfully left school at sixteen to work on his family's ranch full time. He had never been involved in an organized sport at school because the word "school" went along with it, so although he did well in some sports, he couldn't wait to get home and work on the ranch.

Basically, I married a man who partook in such physical activities as hiking up a mountain with sheep, hunting for predators that were preying on his sheep, or making hay for his sheep to feed them in the winter. To him these activities were fun. He had had very few recreational experiences and didn't even know what he liked because he had worked all of his life.

Playing tennis was one of the most wonderful things my husband has ever done with me, because although he knew he was not great at it and probably wouldn't beat me, he still seemed to enjoy letting me teach him. We played on the court in the middle of summer on one of our vacations away from the ranch. We had an absolutely wonderful time, and I treasure that. I realized later that one of my fantasies as a teenager revolved around playing tennis with a boyfriend. Ian had fulfilled my fantasy!

In *His Needs, Her Needs*, Dr. Willard Harley explains that a couple needs fifteen hours a week alone together with no other family, friends, or acquaintances—that's right, *fifteen hours!*

If a husband seriously wants to meet his wife's need to feel close to him, he will give the task sufficient time and attention. I tell male clients they should learn to set aside as much as fifteen hours a week to give their wives undivided attention. Many men look at me as if they think I'm losing my mind, or they just laugh and say, "In other words, I need a thirty-six-hour day." I don't bat an eye, but simply ask them how much time they spent giving their wives undivided attention during their courting days. Any bachelor who fails to devote something close to fifteen hours a week to his girlfriend faces the strong likelihood of losing her.

What happens on a typical dating courtship? A couple finds an activity that provides an excuse to get together. Usually they share a recreational activity, like playing racquetball or going to a movie or out to dinner. But the activity is incidental. They really want to get together to focus on each other. Most dates center around showing each other affection and having conversation.

When a courting couple shares their time, they usually have some basic, although possibly unconscious, goals. They try to get to know each other more thoroughly [and] let each other know how much they care for each other. Why should these goals be dropped after the wedding? The couple desiring a happy marriage carries on with these functions and goals after the wedding. Primarily for the sake of the woman, they must set aside time to have dates with each other. Here's where my recommended fifteen hours comes in. A couple may include sexual interaction in this period of time, but the primary activity should be conversation—private and intimate conversation without children or friends.

When married couples actually get into the habit of doing this, they find fifteen hours about right. Without that much time together, women especially lose the sense of intimacy they need and enjoy so much. And the Love Bank begins to be drained of funds. I have asked many female clients how much time they need with their husbands before they feel close and comfortable enough to enjoy sexual intimacy. More often than not, the answer comes to about fifteen hours a week.

A given activity qualifies to be part of the fifteen-hour goal if you can affirmatively answer the question, "Does this activity allow us to focus primarily on each other?" Going to see a movie for three hours does not meet our criterion. You may exchange some affection during the running of the film, but in most cases you cannot truly say that you focused on each other.

Activities like taking a walk, going to a restaurant, boating on a quiet pond, golfing, sunbathing at the beach—things of that nature—better qualify. Any recreation that requires intense concentration or so much exercise that conversation becomes difficult does not qualify.

If you engaged in conversation while riding together in the car, however, count it toward the fifteen hours. Do the same for shared meals that include no distraction from children or other sources.[15]

I liked this idea, and when I shared it with my husband, he gave a one-sided speech that amounted to, "What husband with five children, running a ranch, pastoring a church has time for fifteen hours alone with his wife? This guy is out of touch with reality!" But as my husband and I began to prove Dr. Harley by

---

[15] Harley, *His Needs, Her Needs.*

trying to schedule those fifteen hours for each other, we found a new passion arising in me and Ian getting more of what he wanted, as well. When we have not made scheduling the fifteen hours with each other a priority, I have found I get more angry and easily annoyed at my husband.

Here is where The Cycle of Intention comes in to play again.

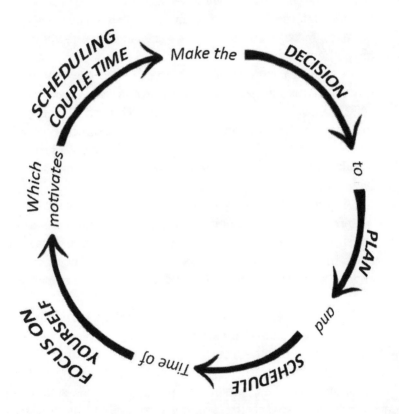

Consider this second example of the difference between planning and scheduling. Steve and Connie sat down one evening in May and agreed to spend some much-needed time together. They thought that a fishing trip on a July weekend sounded pretty good. Steve would have some holiday time then, and they looked forward to it. Steve's brother and wife showed up unannounced for a visit during his time off in July, and soon after Connie's sister begged Connie to help her out with a project that month. Connie said sure and found out two days later that the project would take the rest of their possible holiday time in July. Steve and Connie's plans for their fishing trip were ruined.

That was planning. Now consider the same example with scheduling instead of planning. Steve and Connie sat down one evening in May and agreed to spend some much-needed time together. They thought that a fishing trip on a July weekend sounded pretty good. Steve would have some holiday time then, and they looked forward to it. Steve got out his day planner, confirmed his days off, and circled the third weekend in July for the trip. Connie highlighted the third weekend of July on her kitchen calendar and in her day planner. Steve's brother and wife showed up unannounced during his time off in the beginning of July, and soon after Connie's sister begged Connie to help her out with a project. Connie immediately went to her calendar while speaking to her sister, noticed the highlighted dates, and said, "Sorry, Angie, I am booked for those days and can't possibly change my commitment." Steve also mentioned to his brother as soon as he showed up, "You'll find us rather busy as we are getting ready to take off for the weekend." Steve and Connie's plans for their fishing trip were secured.

The Cycle of Intention is an amazing cycle that you can step into anywhere to begin the journey.

Three Mistakes Couples Sometimes Make When Choosing Their Fifteen Hours

1. My husband and I have often been under the illusion that if we could just watch the right romantic, exciting movie, it would set the mood. It doesn't. If there is ever a passion killer, it is TV. It distracts people from each other. It steals time from intimacy.

Yes, we have had some really enjoyable times cuddling up together and watching a movie or some other favorite show, but it is not a good bedtime activity for creating sexual passion. We are deluded into thinking that this will set the mood for us to relax and feel something for each other. It is an illusion. And yet we try over and over because it is the easiest thing to do.

I'm sure you have heard the good advice that there should be no TV in the bedroom. And yet the majority of master bedrooms I have looked into all have a TV. I have raised seven children and nursed them when they suffered from the influenza or sprained ankles. The TV in our large master bedroom has served us well. It keeps the rest of the household away from the sickly. It gives the ill person privacy when there are visitors. I really appreciate the TV in the privacy of my bedroom when I am sick. And I love getting into bed, getting all cozy, grabbing the remote, and choosing a favorite show to watch at the end of my day. It is my time. I finally have control of something. I want everyone to leave me alone. But twenty minutes into the show, I am fighting sleep! Don't you just hate it when you have tortured yourself to stay awake, only to drift off during the last ten minutes and miss the ending of a good murder mystery?

But if left to this illusion, I would turn on the TV every night thinking it worked for me. Whether I would fall asleep or not, I would become addicted to watching the screen. I realized that once the TV went on, Ian wouldn't be near me because he couldn't get into what I wanted to watch. Since I would fall asleep shortly after I turned the TV on, what was I even getting out of it? The only thing I was getting was the first twenty minutes of feeling in control. It wasn't really working for me or my relationship with my husband.

I realized that what I was looking for was a little time for myself. But I also realized I needed a diversion from the TV. It is so easy to turn it on and relax. I started lighting about ten tall candles in front of my dresser mirror every night (it gives the illusion of a multitude of candles) before slipping into bed. I make sure I have an interesting book within reach. I spend my ten minutes of alone time reading before Ian hops into bed.

Let me insert a point of reality here. At present, in my life, there is always an entourage of teens saying good-night and asking about plans for the next day. They see the candlelit room and fall on the chaise lounge to chat a little longer. They like the ambiance of the room and often will say, "Oh, Mom, can we stay in here for a while? It is so nice!"

"Isn't it?" I say with a smile. "But it is for Dad and me. So enjoy it for two minutes, and then out you go!"

With the television turned off and candles burning, Ian feels welcome because I am not focused on the TV. I may be engrossed in a book, but he says it is different. He gets into bed and picks up where he left off the night before in his book. Then we chitchat about what we are reading.

In this mode we are much more likely to get cuddly, focus on each other, and make love. If there is no lovemaking, we still get an hour of being together, which adds to the fifteen hours and builds up our passion for another time. Time spent alone together is a huge factor for romance and sexual passion.

2. Looking at pornographic material is a way that some couples get excited sexually. Although this can work for a couple temporarily, it is a slippery slope. From what most couples tell me and what I have read about this method, it is my understanding that it does not work forever. One person eventually becomes addicted and has to look at more hard core pornography to get excited for his or her spouse or just chooses to masturbate while looking at the material instead of sharing a fulfilling sex life.

If you truly want to know the truth about pornography and are honest enough to check it out, I highly recommend you read *Truth Behind the Fantasy of Porn: The Greatest Illusion on Earth* by Shelley Lubben.

3. Another mistake some couples make when scheduling their fifteen hours is when one spouse decides to use it for solving

conflict. Do not use the scheduled fifteen hours for solving conflicts! Plan other times for conflict management. When you and your husband were a new couple growing attracted to each other, you didn't use dates or going out to a nice dinner as a time for problem solving. Your husband will not increase his efforts to cherish you if he knows that you are going to use this time to discuss a problem in your relationship, and doing so will likely end with both of you being upset and hurt.

Problems definitely need to be solved, but these scheduled fifteen hours are not for that.

Free Bonus: Go to http://www.marriagebuilders.com/mb2.cfm?recno=14&sublink=358   to download a free Recreational Enjoyment Inventory Form.

10

The Rest of the Story

ALTHOUGH THIS BOOK is not written distinctly for any one faith, in my personal life I have chosen the Christian Bible as my authority for what God is saying to me. In struggling to find out more about how to be sexually fulfilled, almost twenty years ago I came across a verse in the Bible where the apostle Paul said, "[Husbands and wives]...do not deprive each other [sexually] except by mutual consent..." (1 Cor. 7:5).* I thought, "How can a wife who is not getting sexually fulfilled give and keep on giving sexually to her husband if she doesn't feel fulfilled or desire the act?" The God I have come to know in the Bible is loving and kind. I just couldn't believe that he would teach women to *never* say no to a sexual experience with their husband.

I thought that there had to be more said about marital relationships than that. So I began to study more scriptures. I came across the letter written to people who lived in a city called Ephesus in Greece. Paul, a man of God, writes, "Husbands, love

---

* New International Version

your wives, just as Christ loved the church and gave himself up for her...." (Eph. 5:25).* Now that is more like it! Christ would never force the church (his body) to engage in a service that was distasteful. And a woman who has not been sexually fulfilled and has low sexual desire could quite often find the act of sexual intercourse distasteful.

This led me to another letter written by Paul to a younger pastor called Titus. In the letter, it says that the older women are to "...train the younger women to love their husbands..." (Titus 2:4).** The Greek word for love in this passage means "as a woman loves a man." I realized that that meant sexually, and it sounded like there was actually something that women were supposed to pass on to other women. That was something I was looking for. It didn't mean that older women were supposed to just tell a woman how to engage in the sexual act in marriage—after all, a couple could figure that out by themselves. However, it did mean that older, experienced, wiser women were supposed to train the younger women on how to "sexually love" their husbands. The older women were supposed to take the initiative, not by forcing the younger women to take a course, but by being available in a visible way.

Then I found something written by the apostle Peter: "You husbands likewise, live with your wives in an understanding way... and grant her honor as a fellow-heir of the grace of life, so that your prayers may not be hindered" (1 Peter 3:7).** I had never heard the phrase *"so that your prayers may not be hindered"* spoken about. I have always been interested in finding out exactly what words mean, so I began to dig and study what the following phrases actually mean in the original Greek that they were written in: "understanding way," "grant her honor," and "may not be hindered."

---

* New International Version
** New American Standard Version
** New American Standard Version

The rest of the passage was fairly clear to me, but I wanted to find out what those three phrases really meant. This is what I found out (please note that the italics below are mine):

1. "You husbands likewise, live with your wives in an *understanding way*" (meaning: as in science; understand them physically and emotionally and act accordingly).
2. "and *grant her honor...*" (meaning: cherish her).
3. "*may not be hindered...*" (meaning: frustrate or cut in on; as taking an axe to the base of a tree).

The conclusion is that if men do not learn what it is their wives need both emotionally and physically in the marital relationship and fail to rise to meet that need, they might as well not even pray to God for anything. They will have no prayer power. On the other hand, if a man loves his wife unselfishly, cherishes her, and meets her emotional and physical needs, she wouldn't want to deprive him of anything.

When I discovered how important it is for a woman to be cherished, I began to realize how critical it is for a woman to understand herself, understand what makes her feel cherished, and articulate this to her husband. This is serious stuff, and I became passionate about sharing it with other women. At this point, I'm sure female readers are asking, "Why are you telling us this? This should be told to our husbands." And again I will say that when I write a book for men, I will tell them the same thing, but who better to help a husband understand what makes his wife feel cherished than his wife?

This chapter is being included in this book to motivate women to not give up on understanding what makes them feel cherished and to share this with their husband so that their husbands can then respond to their needs. What woman wouldn't want her husband's prayers to be answered when he is asking God for wisdom to raise his children with character, enough income to care for their needs, success in the new job, and the ability *to understand his wife and meet her needs*? Wouldn't a woman want to help her husband understand her needs and remind (not nag) him to do so so that his prayers are not cut off?

As your husband's partner, you have a responsibility to see this through. It is very easy to throw up your hands and quit trying to improve the communication in this area when your partner is not being responsive. Who said a hot, sexy marriage was easy? It is not easy, but it is worth it! It all depends on whether you want it or not.

11

Do You Really Want It?

ASHLEY HAS AN excellent soccer organization in her community. She thought that her children were missing out on socializing and sports. Soccer practice was twice a week. Her husband, Jack, didn't finish work until after the start of soccer practice, and there was no one else close by whom she could trust to drive her children, so she decided with her husband that she would begin driving their children, aged six to twelve, to soccer.

It wasn't long before she discovered this was the farthest thing from healthy family time than she had imagined. By the time they had gotten all the equipment together, something in their tummies, and everything organized for four children and a mother to drive twenty-five minutes, at least half of them were in a bad mood. To top it all off, not everything that happened at soccer was wonderful for the children. Although there was some physical benefit, Ashley realized that this wasn't really improving her family time. They weren't growing closer together, and it certainly was taking away time that she could have spent with her husband.

These are the things you have to consider by comparing the pros and cons. Women might say they want a better sex life with their husbands, but do they really? Are they really willing to take up the challenge and say no to things that their neighbors or best friends are taking their kids to? Are they willing to say no to their good friends when personally asked to be a part of a hockey or curling team or to participate in some kind of quilting marathon?

Everyone needs to be involved with things they are passionate about, but too much of a "good thing" does not always benefit the very relationships that they hold so dear. It is of top importance to clarify your belief system, protect that system with parameters, know your limits, and plan your life out accordingly.

There are so many good things you could be doing. There are so many good things that you could be taking your children to and have them involved with, but in the end too many good things often end up being the pressure that cause ill health in a family, sometimes even breaking a family apart.

You need to identify the factors in your life that are blocking your sexual passion. It usually has to do with time. As I have already said, TV takes away time that could be spent with your spouse. Less time spent together communicating and recreating leads to less sexual desire. Dealing with jam-packed children's schedules and enforcing children's bedtime routines are other issues to deal with. Visit www.silkonfirebook. com to see my free bonus video, "Tips for Parents: Children's Bedtime Routine". Another factor is a person's inability to say no to volunteering for good causes in the community. It is good to volunteer for projects that you are passionate about in your community, your children's schools, or your church. You might have a helping spirit, which is wonderful, but don't let that snowball into spending hours a week involved with these projects. A person with a spouse/family has to be very, very careful. I actually believe that if 50 percent of married couples in a community decided to change their ways and up their sex drives, 50 percent less community and extracurricular activities would be needed. These things only exist because good people say yes to helping out with such projects. If people were more concerned about their relationships and upping their sex drives with their mates, perhaps there would be less need for all these extracurricular things.

Your life habits will have to change if you really want it; if you really want to crave sex with your husband more than you do now, you will have to change. There's no doubt about it. You can't keep doing the same thing that you've been doing and expect to get different results.

In Summary

1. Learn how to achieve orgasm (chapter 2).
2. Understand the motor (feeling cherished) that drives your sexual desire (chapter 4).
3. Make it a priority to schedule time to focus in on yourself as a sensuous, hot, sexy woman (chapter 8).
4. Learn how to communicate the above to your husband (chapter 4).
5. Begin scheduling in fifteen hours per week with your husband (chapter 9).

It is very important to successfully focus in on yourself as a hot, sexy woman because this will speak volumes to your spouse about your credibility. He will then believe that you truly do want to grow in your sexual craving for him and will be less likely to feel like you are finding fault with the way he responds to you at present when you discuss your needs with him (the fourth item on the list).

The question is, "Do you really want it?" If you do, you will have to actually write down what you're going to do to change. You need to discipline yourself to:

- Focus on yourself weekly to be a sexual woman.
- Schedule the time to focus.
- Schedule time for you and your husband to be together, not just for lovemaking, but for those fifteen hours of being alone together and doing something that you both enjoy.
- Effectively communicate with your husband.
- Plan time to communicate with him in a nonjudgmental way.
- Communicate with teenagers in the home about their schedule. You cannot keep up with the schedule you have been on. You have to remove something from your schedule, and if it's driving the children certain places, you'll have to take a good hard look at what activities you will have to cut down on.

Will the children like it? No, but in the end they will. Your marriage will be stronger, you will be less vulnerable to a divorce, and the children will have a more secure home life. You have to ask yourself whether you want a secure home life for the children. Or are you too scared of disappointing them in the short-term and fearful of them not liking you and arguing with you when you put your foot down about driving them to certain activities? If you have young children, now is a good time to have a conversation with your husband about how involved you are going to allow your children to be with extracurricular activities during the week.

You need to decide whether you really want to crave sex with your husband and up your sexual drive. No one person can do everything. You will have to decide what your philosophy is and what your belief system is for your home life. This will drive and motivate what you schedule in. Are you really motivated to take the time to sit down and decide what activities you're going to change and what habits you're going to develop? If not, there's no sense in blaming anything or anybody but yourself.

If you want it, you *can* have it; you *can* do something about it. You now have a guide to teach you how to achieve orgasm, feel cherished and stay attracted to your husband. Use the summary to review the steps, take action and I am confident that you will begin to crave sex with your husband and continue to desire him more.

Notes

1. Dr. Willard F. Harley Jr., in discussion with the author, 1998.
2. Lori and Paul Byerly, "The Female Genitals," The Marriage Bed, accessed May 11, 2013, http://site.themarriagebed.com/biology/her-plumbing.
3. Ibid.
4. *World Book Dictionary*, 1986 ed., s.v. "cherish.".
5. Dr. Willard F. Harley Jr., "The Question of the Ages: How Can a Husband Receive the Sex He Needs in Marriage?," Marriage Builders, accessed May 14, 2013, http://www.marriagebuilders.com/graphic/mbi8120_sex.html.
6. Ibid.
7. Paddy Ducklow, in discussion with the author, February, 2008.
8. Dr. Phil McGraw, *Dr. Phil*, Culver City, CA: Columbia Tristar Entertainment.
9. Harley, "The Question of the Ages."
10. Allan Dunbar, in discussion with the author, (1980?).
11. Dr. Willard F. Harley Jr., *His Needs, Her Needs* (Tarrytown: Fleming H. Revell Company, 1986).

12. Dr. Emerson Eggerichs, *Love & Respect: The Love She Most Desires, The Respect He Desperately Needs* (Brentwood: Integrity Publishers, 2004).

13. *Curiosity.com*, "What is Neuroplasticity?," http://curiosity.discovery.com/question/what-is-neuroplasticity (accessed August 8, 2012).

14. *Wikipedia*, "Neuroplasticity," http://en.wikipedia.org/wiki/Neuroplasticity (accessed August 8, 2012).

15. Harley, His Needs, Her Needs.

Recommended reading:

Books:

Catrall, Kim, *Sexual Intelligence* (New York: Little, Brown and Company, 2008).

Eggerichs, Dr. Emerson, *Love & Respect: The Love She Most Desires, The Respect He Desperately Needs* (Brentwood: Integrity Publishers, 2004).

Faye, Erin, *Essential Elements of Sex* (Bloomington: iUniverse,2012).

Harley, Dr. Willard F., Jr., *His Needs, Her Needs* (Tarrytown: Fleming H. Revell Company, 1986).

————, *5 Steps to Romantic Love* (Grand Rapids: Fleming H. Revell, 1993).

McCarthy, Barry and Emily, *Rekindling Desire: A Step-by-Step Program to Help Low-Sex and No-Sex Marriages* (Brunner/ Routledge, 2003).

Articles:

Kaye, Marcia, "Not This Year, Darling: Has Your Sex Life Gone into Permanent Sleep Mode?," Canadian Health, accessed June 18, 2013, http://www.canadian-health.ca/6_3/32_e.html.

Marriage Builders, "How to Overcome Sexual Aversion," accessed June 18, 2013, http://www.marriagebuilders.com/graphic/mbi5047_qa.html.

Karen's Contact Information

To book Karen Moilliet for speaking engagements and
Silk On Fire™ workshops:
karen@silkonfirebook.com
1-250-674-8489

For Passion Coaching:
karen@silkonfirebook.com
www.silkonfirebook.com

For Life Coaching:
karen@lifecoachhelps.com
www.lifecoachhelps.com